THE STONE VILLAGES OF BRITAIN

Contents

Corris

1
Historical Survey

A few miles west of Durham, in the remarkably unexceptional church in the Weardale village of Frosterley, there is a unique memorial. In area little more than the size of this page, a highly polished piece of stone, dark grey and filled with pale-grey fossils, bears an inscription along the bottom two inches of its length:

> This Frosterley marble and limestone,
> quarried for centuries in this parish,
> adorns cathedrals and churches
> throughout the world.

So far as I know, this is the only recorded memorial to a building stone, albeit one restricted to internal use for church pillars, steps, fonts and memorials, particularly in medieval times. Today, chopped and crushed, it is merely a constituent of concrete. A similar fate has befallen many of our finest building stones, although here and there some quarries are still worked, more to provide a supply of stone for restoration purposes than for new houses.

In the past, stone was used almost exclusively for major buildings, cathedrals, churches, castles, monasteries. Wherever it was abundant it was subsequently used for manor-houses and merchants' houses, for markets, guildhalls and bridges, but where wood was more readily available, as it was over most of England until the late sixteenth century, timber was favoured, especially for the far greater number of smaller houses in towns and villages, for farmhouses, barns and cottages. This book is concerned with the use of natural stone as the main building material in villages, creating the *genius loci*, imparting its essential character, appreciated visually through colours, tones and textures.

Inevitably, some lines of definition need to be drawn, if only loosely. From the point of view of size, the village needs to be large enough to have a focal point or centre, such as church, chapel, cross or green, and sufficient other buildings, such as houses, cottages, farms and barns, to form one or more groups, even if haphazardly arranged as so often is the case. A pub is desirable though not essential. There must be a recognisable amount of stone – it will almost certainly be local stone – in the walls of village buildings even though, in some cases, it lies hidden beneath layers of lime or colour-wash. The

7

environment should be rural, although I admit that in some Pennine and other northern areas the overall picture is an urban and industrial one. Finally, the place must 'feel' like a village even if its local importance is that of a small market town. Instinct rather than population count is the guide here. Thus, I regard Chipping Campden, Ribchester and St David's as villages, even at the risk of offending their inhabitants.

Research and discoveries by archaeologists, geographers and historians are showing to an increasing degree that many, probably most, pre-industrial villages are older than was first realised, and that the village as a community is more complex than was usually thought. If villages are individual entities, they share the common factor of having undergone repeated changes. Visually – and that is what this book is mainly concerned with – the greatest changes have occurred within the last twenty-five years. One outcome of these is the paradox that newcomers to the village occupy the older houses, while the older village inhabitants often occupy new council housing. The newcomers, professional people, retired people, commuters, have given their village a face-lift by restoring old property, not always with the sensible restraint and good taste that is desirable. Nevertheless, it is true to say that, apart from their peripheral growth, most villages look far better today than a generation ago, and almost unrecognisably so than they appeared at the turn of the century. There is less decay and dereliction, more fresh paint and newly pointed masonry, and roofs are in a better state of repair.

The house in which I have lived for a number of years lies just outside a fine example of a stone village. Most of the village houses date from the second half of the eighteenth century when local prosperity had peaked, generating a wave of new building or rebuilding. Three-storey houses lining the main street give an almost urban air, and there are many smaller houses, of individual character, but joined in informal terraces. The Old Hall, a Caroline manor-house of 1678, was destroyed by fire in 1935, to be replaced, in stone, by a typical 1930s bay-windowed structure.

Three-quarters of the village houses are owner-occupied, and the rest are tenanted or tied, with only 7 per cent of the housing stock provided by the district council. One-fifth of the occupied housing – that is, 15 per cent of village houses – are used for holiday lets or as second homes, an average percentage for this valley of Wensleydale in the Yorkshire Dales National Park. All the houses are stone-built or stone-faced, and most have stone-slate roofs, and strict planning controls ensure that repairs, restoration or the very limited amount of new building must maintain the stone character of the village.

(opposite)

Geddington, Northamptonshire. Eleanor Cross, 1294, of Weldon stone, at the heart of a beautiful limestone village

My own house, a former farmhouse of about 1700, has a history of continual development, with at least eight identifiable changes between 1700 and 1970, representing a change almost every generation. The building has grown lineally, like other dales' farmhouses, and although stone-flagged floors survive some have been concreted or boarded over. The main changes have been in the increase in comfort to conform with contemporary tastes. I have little doubt that the families who lived here in the middle of last century, when it was two separate houses, would still recognise the building both outside and inside. The occupants of fifty years earlier would also find a degree of familiarity, but the house of *c*1750 was much smaller, much lower and probably had a roof of ling thatch.

A house of stone may change, but it, like a stone village, is really irreplaceable. I am constantly aware of this factor, a feeling shared with my friends in the village. We know we are fortunate to live in a place to which stone contributes so much character. Admittedly, the surroundings of stone-walled fields, stone barns and farms, and the friendly hills with their clean, challenging skylines play their part, but I am sure that we are conscious, if only silently, of the harmony between our homes and their environment.

A stone village is an agglomeration, either having grown naturally over centuries or having been planned at one time by one landlord. Occupants of the stone houses and cottages would share one feature common to all stone houses – they are cold to live in. External walls are likely to be between 18in (45cm) and 3ft (1m) thick (mine average out at just 2ft (61cm)) and internal ones rather less than this. Some partitions may be of wood or brick. An external appearance of comfortable snug solidity can be misleading, for without good heating, stone houses are cool in summer and cold in winter. If heated well, and with heat losses minimised, they can be cosy throughout the year. It is easy to admire the colour and texture of stonework in villages from Cornwall to the Cotswolds and to Caithness, perhaps to envy the people who live in buildings of such apparent solidity and permanence, but it needs to be stated again that present appearance is the result of improvements made most likely since the 1950s, possibly much later still.

I lived for twenty-five years in a stone village just across the Wiltshire border from Bath. It did not take me long to become aware of the fine quality of domestic buildings which characterised villages and small towns in the immediate neighbourhood, or as I travelled around to see the subtle changes in colour and texture, even within a few miles. If a journey took me southwestwards, the pale creamy-grey oolite of village houses near Bath soon gave way to the cold grey-white limestone in villages on Mendip – Farmborough, High Littleton, and Ston Easton – to be replaced by brick and cob across the Somerset fenlands. If the Fosse Way was then followed towards Ilminster, it revealed the honey-gold stones in the villages around Montacute and the Hamdons; a few miles westwards led to the cool greys of the Curry villages near

Somerton, and if the route continued beyond Taunton and along the foot of the Quantocks, warm pinky-russets prevailed at Bishop's Lydeard and Crow-combe to be replaced by more rugged, slaty stones of darker colours and poorer quality on the Brendon Hills and Exmoor. Thus, a cross-country journey of 60 miles (96km) lasting a couple of hours revealed at least six different types of stone used in village housing. It also showed a marked variation in building styles.

Contrasting with this was a journey roughly orientated north-north-eastwards from Bath, keeping close company with the Fosse Way again. For the same length of time and distance as before – two hours or about 60 miles (96km) – I would be on the Jurassic Limestone all the way. Village after village showed remarkable similarities in their houses, the only difference being in setting, size and scale. This journey embraced Cotswold country, where vernacular building in stone flowered as nowhere else in Britain between the last quarter of the sixteenth century and the early part of the eighteenth, and continued to flourish for the best part of the next hundred years.

These examples of quite short journeys of roughly equal length, made from the same starting point but travelling in opposite directions, show in small scale what, as a whole, Britain offers in the larger compass. If you travel from Dover north-westwards across England and Wales to Holyhead, you will cross at least a dozen different types of rocks, formed at different times, each creat-ing different landscapes, with different building materials in villages and farms, not all of them of stone. If, on the other hand, you started at Lyme Regis in Dorset and navigated an intricate course to Lincoln, thence to the Humber Bridge, and northwards almost to the mouth of the Tees near Middlesbrough, you would be on only one main rock formation, that of the Jurassic period. Landscapes would have much more similarity and serenity, though local differences would still occur. Farms and village houses reflect the unity of materials along this Jurassic belt of rock.

Nothing illustrates this better than the Geological Survey Ten Mile Map, which covers the whole of Britain in two sheets, North and South, the division being roughly along the line Ravenglass–Windermere–Catterick to the York-shire coast between Scarborough and Whitby. The map shows in a range of clear colours the 'solid geology' of the land, that is, the principal rocks beneath the surface. It also shows main roads, principal towns and villages, rivers but not contours, and not counties. As a guide to what you might expect to find, so far as local building materials are concerned, it is invaluable. I think it also happens to be a beautiful piece of cartography, the choice of some of its colours showing a touch of genius. The band of oolitic limestone which runs from Dorset to Yorkshire is pale yellow, its neighbouring Lias almost orange, while the Mountain Limestone of Mendip, Derbyshire and the Yorkshire Dales is shown as pale blue. Chalk country of Wessex, the downs, Chilterns and wolds is appropriately grass-green, and areas of bright red indicate the indestructible, unyielding granites of Cornwall, Devon and the Lake District. The North sheet, which includes the whole of Scotland, is quite startlingly magnificent in vivid colours, a fair indication of stunning scenery but poor quality domestic buildings.

The importance of geology cannot be over-emphasised. It is fundamental in shaping our lives. Rocks and the topography they create determine what vegetation will grow and hence what livestock this can support. They determine whether a community will flourish as a result of mineral resources, and, in giving the land its basic shape and structure, rocks also influence the routes of communication. So far as this book is concerned, rocks provide the stone for village buildings, but of all the types of rock available in Britain two principal ones only are responsible for probably ninety out of every hundred stone-built or stone-faced houses, limestone and sandstone. Of the other building stones, granite, slate and flint play a very minor role, although it is one which should not be overlooked completely.

Good as it is, however, the Geological Survey Ten Mile Map alone will not guarantee an accurate assessment of what local village building materials may be. Few rock formations, though shown in a single colour, are necessarily consistent throughout their range. Rocks are classified according to when they were formed and not on their physical structure. Thus, although the Jurassic Limestones are more consistent than most formations, they do reveal local characteristics, especially in colour and granular structure, some being very fine grained, others more shelly, while in North Yorkshire they are so sandy that there is a division of opinion as to whether they are sandy limestones or calcareous sandstones. Limestones of the Lias beds are much more subject to greater colour variations through different mineral content, particularly iron. Equally, some areas shown on the map where limestone may be expected have alluvial deposits of clay which have proved suitable for brick-making.

At all times it needs to be remembered that stone was the most prestigious and expensive building material, not so much in its cost at the quarry as in the cost of transporting it. Not until the canal age of the late eighteenth century and the first half of the nineteenth, and the railway age which overlapped and then overtook it, did the cost of transport become less important than that of the raw material. Thus, apart from its use in the construction of major buildings, stone for village houses and farms was obtained from local quarries and travelled the least possible distance to its site of use. It is this extremely local use of stone which results in sharp changes in 'village-scapes' often within very short distances. Villages on the edge of stone belts may include a variety of materials. Lacock in Wiltshire is one of the most beautiful and frequently visited of National Trust villages. Lying on the coarse Cornbrash Limestone with the oolite immediately to the west and the Oxford Clay to the east, its main buildings – Lacock Abbey, its tithe barns and the parish church – are of oolitic limestone. At the Dissolution of the Monasteries some of the Lacock

Abbey stone went into village housing; other houses and cottages of the seventeenth and eighteenth centuries have Cornbrash in their walls. A few houses are half-timbered, one with cruck framing with brick and plaster infill; there are some Georgian brick houses, as well as Victorian and modern ones. Although Lacock shows a mixture of materials, stone predominates. Exuberant details and steep-sided gables rising above adjoining, lichened stone-slate roofs anticipate the Cotswold idiom a few miles to the north.

To return to the Geological Survey Map. The band of pale yellow which marks the Jurassic rocks also represents an important frontier, for it divides Britain into two zones, Highland and Lowland. South and east of it lies Lowland Britain, the land of the newer and softer rocks, all of them sedimentary – chalk, clays, softer sandstones and alluvial deposits – none of them yielding satisfactory building stones. To the north and west of the Jurassic line and including it, is Highland Britain, incorporating about half of England, together with the whole of Wales and Scotland. These are the areas of the older rocks and the further to the north and west you go the harder and older the rocks become, yielding a variety of stones suitable for building use. So the broad generalisation may be made that villages predominantly of stone are more likely to be found in the Highland zone than in the Lowland zone.

Lacock, Wiltshire. On the edge of the limestone. Main buildings: barn of stone; some houses of stone; half-timbering on a stone base

Another factor arises, however. History and economic conditions have also played their part in determining the nature of village buildings. Thus, from medieval times to early last century, the gentle uplands of the Jurassic Limestone belt have been a source of wealth based largely on sheep, and to a lesser degree on quarrying. But this prosperity did not occur at the same times in every part of the area and this variation in dates of local affluence is reflected in the different period styles of building, although it embodied similar techniques in the use of stone. In the higher, wilder landscapes of the Pennines there was no comparable accumulation of wealth through wool and when the rebuilding of village houses in stone did take place, generally from the mid-seventeenth century onwards, they tended to be more modest in appearance, but with an austerity of character completely in harmony with their environment.

Stone villages belong mainly, though not exclusively, to upland Britain. But the older and harder the rocks become the higher and wilder are the hills, and, generalising again, the poorer is the land, the more sparsely situated its villages; as the chapters on Wales and Scotland will show, village housing there is generally inferior to that along England's limestone belt. One reason for this is, of course, that in regions such as Cornwall, the Lake District, North Wales and the Highlands, the available stone was not sedimentary, which can be easily quarried and shaped, but igneous in origin, very hard and intractable. So use was made of whatever stone was handiest, boulders lying on the surface or washed down by streams and rivers. Only the most rudimentary shaping of such material being possible, houses built of it look crude and rough by comparison with those constructed of more serviceable stone. Even in those favoured limestone areas where there was a good 'freestone', that is, one which could be sawn to give a smooth surface, usually called ashlar, this type of finish was frequently forgone because of its extra cost. As a result, the material was used in walling as coursed rubble, imparting to the masonry a rough-textured surface pleasantly contrasting with ashlared quoins, and with the smooth-surfaced stones of other houses in the same village.

In areas where the old hard rocks prevail, the native granites and slates when used as building stones often have their gritty, dour appearance obscured by a surface rendering with the application of whitewash or colour-wash. It is this bright colouring which doubtless explains the visual appeal of so many Cornish villages, especially when, as so often is the case, it is reflected in the gently lapping waters of a sheltered harbour. Although the stone is hidden you know it is present, so there is no justification for excluding such villages from

(opposite)_____
Polperro, Cornwall. Whitewashed stone enhanced by a water-front setting

Bainbridge, North Yorkshire. Stone houses and cottages around a large green: individually unexceptional, outstanding as a group

14

this survey. Indeed, were I to do so, Wales and Scotland would have very few representatives. Surface painting is also to be found in areas where the Old Red and New Red Sandstones have been used in village buildings, for these materials are not always resistant to weathering and extra protection is desirable. The older sandstones and gritstones of the Pennines need no such protection, nor do the limestones of the Jurassic belt, and it is those regions more than any other where the native stone has produced villages which belong completely to their surroundings having, almost literally, grown from them. The use of local materials may have been guided by necessity but the unconscious result is a perfect visual harmony, and villages resemble extended outcrops from local quarries.

As I look out of the window from my house on a south-facing hillside above a Wensleydale village in the Yorkshire Dales National Park, every building I see, with the exception of one or two hideous modern farm buildings which planning laws are powerless to prevent, is of local stone, a grey-brown sandstone used in houses, cottages, farms, barns and walls. Every roof is of heavy stone slabs, its pitch echoing that of distant hillsides. Yet there is no uniformity or monotony. Subtle variations in colour and texture of stone ensures that. Different types of sandstone have been used for the masonry of walls, for lintels, for quoins, for flagstones on the floor, for a staircase, and every piece of stone in the house has been quarried and brought to the site. No records exist of sources and the land nearby shows little visual evidence of quarrying, yet the result represents an enormous amount of human endeavour and physical toil, allied to much skill and craftsmanship.

This is for only one building. Multiply it a hundredfold, a thousandfold, for all the houses and villages in the area. Multiply this again many, many times for the houses and villages in all the other stone areas of Britain and you begin to get an inkling of the effort and expertise that has given us the stone heritage of buildings in the Highland zone of Britain. Very little written evidence exists to throw light on methods and costs of construction of houses and cottages in our stone villages or of work at the quarries which yielded the stone. Certainly in those areas where good stone was abundant, almost every village or township had its own quarry. Today, these can be identified on the ground as overgrown hollows or as the curving sweeps of low outcrops often beautified naturally by brightly coloured flowers which have taken root and established themselves on old workings. Surface quarries were generally shallow, suitable stone in the Jurassic belt occurring only a few feet below the ground. In some quarries, notably between Bath and Corsham, at Chilmark in Wiltshire, and in the Isle of Purbeck, the stone was mined by way of horizontal galleries from a hillside, which allowed quarrymen to tackle the well-bedded stones at the base of a good stratum. Throughout much of the last century huge quantities of oolitic limestone were obtained thus, while in my own particular part of upper Wensleydale sandstone was similarly mined. Some stone mines had working faces as much as 50 or 60ft (15 or 18m) beneath the surface. Monk's Park Quarry near Corsham, Wiltshire, first worked in 1872, now extends over about 40 acres (16ha) and has its freestone – the major present source of Bath stone – nearly 100ft (30m) underground.

Old large-scale maps, either the early Ordnance Survey Six-Inch, or the tithe maps of a parish, often give the documentary clue to quarries, with 'Township Quarry', 'Poor Persons' Quarry', 'Quarry Field' or 'Stone Pit Lane', names still existing in many villages. The workings have long been abandoned, but their stone, 'the aristocrat of building materials', as Mr Alec Clifton-Taylor so succinctly describes it, survives in the houses, cottages and farms of hundreds of villages.

As Dr Brunskill has pointed out, with special reference to vernacular buildings in any community, but particularly in villages, the type and size of building varies with social status and time. So far as English stone villages are concerned, the church and castle will be medieval, the manor-house medieval down to the sixteenth century, yeomen's or substantial farmers' houses seventeenth century, the homes of merchants and professional people eighteenth century, while labourers, artisans, quarrymen and miners would live in nineteenth-century cottages. While this is certainly an over-simplification, it serves as a guide to dates, types and numbers of houses of different sizes.

Bamburgh, Northumberland. Village and castle in harmony

In most stone villages there are likely to be far more cottages of late eighteenth- and nineteenth-century date than there are larger houses of the seventeenth and eighteenth centuries. Only in the wool-prosperous Cotswolds is this proportion likely to be different, for there a greater middle-class and merchant prosperity resulted in large numbers of fine seventeenth- and eighteenth-century houses, and relatively fewer artisans' cottages. To a large extent, it is this variation in proportions of house types and sizes and their lay-out in the rural scene which makes for village identity, and also explains why estate villages or industrial villages of one build, though socially and historic-ally interesting, lack the contrasts which most villages enjoy, and which are the product of centuries of growth.

Villages of all types have changed in response to changing needs, either nationally or locally. Only occasionally are we vouchsafed glimpses of what they were like in the past, through the writings of early travellers. In 1698 Celia Fiennes found at Land's End that : 'the houses are but poor cottages like barns to look on, much like those in Scotland – but to doe my own County its right the inside of their little cottages are clean and plaister'd, and such as you might comfortably eat and drink there . . .' Writing a century earlier, Richard Carew describes old Cornish cottages as having 'walles of earth, low thatched roofs, few partitions, no planchings or glass windows, and scarcely any chimneys, other than a hole in the wall to let out smoke.' In the Lake District, Celia Fiennes saw villages

> of sad, little hutts made up of drye walls, only stones piled together and the roofs of same slatt; there seemed to be little or noe tunnells for their chimneys and have no mortar or plaister within or without; for the most part I took them at first sight for a sort of houses or barns to fodder cattle in, not thinking them to be dwelling-houses . . . in some places there may be 20 or 30 together.

This must have been quite a large village for seventeenth-century Lakeland.

Villages can be appreciated at different levels, both as dynamic rural com-munities and as collections of various houses and other buildings. Although this survey of stone villages concentrates on the physical and visual aspect, the life within the villages should not be ignored. Except for those of the squire, large landowner, and often the parson, almost every village dwelling is itself a record of the changing lifestyle of its earlier occupants, their affluence or poverty, their aspirations and fears, and the ebb and flow of village life under the influence of external social factors.

Profound changes occurred during the eighteenth century which had great effect on village life. In the earlier decades, when towns were expanding and using the products of the countryside, cottagers in many villages enjoyed more relative prosperity than ever before – but this was only a short-lived boom, for the Enclosure Acts which proliferated and peaked from about 1750 onwards, though paving the way for better and more prosperous farming, markedly weakened the village. Farmers tended to move out from their village homes into new farmhouses set in the middle of their newly enclosed fields. Lower down the social scale, cottagers with rights of common grazing were not compensated for loss of these, and squatters on the wastes and commons, living a breadline existence on casual labour, were faced with eviction. Writing in 1912 George Bourne thought that 'To the enclosure of the common more than to any other cause may be traced all the changes that have subsequently passed over the village'. One outcome of the enclosures was to reduce thousands of squatters and cottagers to the status of landless labourers, many of whom migrated to the growing towns.

In many 'closed' villages where the parish was owned by one landlord, or at most by a very small number, cottages were demolished or allowed to decay. In 'open' villages the landless labourers frequently found themselves forced to live in empty farmhouses or barns converted into cottages, while new cottages erected by small tradesmen were let to these labourers at high rents. Cottage rows or terraces appeared in the scene towards the end of the eighteenth century, either for these agricultural labourers or for the workers attracted by new local industries – quarrying, mining, textiles.

In 'open' villages, those who could afford to do so employed a builder, and even then, for any work involving detail such as lintels and mullions, a mason may have been used. Cottagers and other poorer folk built their own houses, an activity which was often a communal affair, particularly in the remoter and less sophisticated parts of the country such as Cornwall and northern England. Stone is the most dense of all building materials, the sandstones, gritstones and granites being especially 'numb'. Raising them into the size and shape of a house would present a daunting prospect, single-handed, and is one where, so far as the smaller houses and cottages are concerned, very little documentary evidence exists to give a detailed picture.

However, from the last quarter of the eighteenth century some accounts exist giving details of cottage building. Emparking by landowners and the resultant creation of 'model' villages brought in professional designers and architects, who published pattern books, although the designs in these had little effect on subsequent building. The houses continued to be occupied by the poorest people, described by Nathaniel Kent in 1775 as in such disrepair that wind and rain penetrated everywhere, which meant the one room used by a man, his wife and family for living, eating and sleeping. Generally speaking, the standards of these cottages declined the further north one went.

At about the end of the eighteenth century an estate cottage with a principal downstairs room, and smaller pantry, and two bedrooms upstairs, and a half-acre of land, would cost around £60. A pair of flint-walled cottages in Norfolk built in 1810 cost £130, each having a 15 × 11ft (4.5 × 3.3m) living-room with a loft bedroom and smaller bedroom above. Only the living-room had a window. A single flint cottage for one family had a 12ft sq (3.6m sq) living-room, two smaller rooms adjoining and a chamber above, and cost £40, and would be let for 3 guineas a year. Dorset cottages at the same time, with two ground-floor rooms and two above in the roof space cost between £60 and £80, and would be let for 5 or 6 guineas a year, that is, around 2s a week. An agricultural labourer's wage of 1s a day – certainly not more than 1s 6d a day – are best judged in terms of what they would buy. The rector of Barkham, a Dorset village, calculated the weekly budget for a local family of six, in 1795, as between 8s and 9s. Thus, with a weekly rental of at least 2s to meet, a labourer's wage would not always be sufficient to cover living costs. It became sheer necessity for older children to go out to work, even at 3d a day. Almost a century later, in an agricultural village in Berkshire, the situation was little different. The father earned 10s a week and one of the seven children was at work earning half this; household food and essentials cost nearly 13s, and the cottage rent was 1s 6d. There was very little to spare, so any chance of supplementing it was welcomed; and the temptation to move to the industrial towns for better paid employment was very great.

Throughout the country, but especially in northern counties, the artisan population expanded rapidly during the eighteenth and nineteenth centuries. Villages in the West Riding and Lancashire textile areas had increased numbers of weavers, while lead-miners and, later, coal-miners almost began to outnumber agricultural labourers. There was a great demand for more houses, a need met by employers, landlords and the workers themselves, usually by the quickest and cheapest methods. Old hovels were patched up, rebuilt, or replaced by stone terraces. Tofts in the village street had new cottages built on them, creating almost continuous street frontages. This is why in so many villages there is such a variety of house types and sizes, the outstanding and the insignificant mixed together, a community of buildings and people, largely a rent-paying community in past centuries but now far more likely to be a house-owning one.

When mill-owners provided workers' housing they usually adopted the minimum standard, a one-roomed cottage, although some two-storey ones were erected, too. Miners' cottages of the early nineteenth century in northern pit villages were similar, but with a bedroom in the roof space. In Northumberland and the Border counties, the one-roomed single labourer's bothy was common, with single-storey terraces for married labourers, all contrasting with farmhouses described by Cobbett as 'big enough and fine enough for a gentleman to live in'.

Although single-storey cottages were universally common during the nineteenth century, the further north you go the more dominant they continue to be. In Scotland, outside the industrial regions, it was not until the second half of the century that the now familiar two-storey house, usually with its upper windows gabled, appeared on the scene. The single-storey Scottish cottage differed from the traditional 'black houses' mainly in having windows, fireplaces at the gables, and a higher, wider, tiled or slated roof. Inside, the one or two rooms would have box-beds, and even this tradition continued occasionally when the one-and-a-half- or two-storey houses were built. My experience of box-beds in my son's house in the north of Scotland is that they are practical, cosy and comfortable.

Stone may seem to be the most indestructible of building materials, but it will not last for ever. Nevertheless, one can hope with some confidence that the stone houses and villages in which we are fortunate enough to live should at least see us through our own lifetimes and probably those of the next few generations. The appeal of villages in general, and stone ones in particular, to urban dwellers is resulting in increasing numbers of people moving to those same rural areas deserted gradually over the past two generations. New residents in stone villages are not only prepared to 'do up' their old stone houses and cottages – though not always in good taste – and can afford to do so. Indeed, listed building or conservation area status enjoyed by many villages as a means of protecting the architectural heritage makes possible the provision of grants towards preserving or enhancing the appearance or character of individual buildings or groups of buildings.

Unhappily, the converse sometimes applies. Where district councils are not sufficiently strict, new buildings are erected which are unsympathetic in materials, structure or design, and too often these create a tasteless accretion on the edge of an otherwise harmonious stone village. Not all council housing is bad, and I can think of some rural examples which are of a remarkably high standard, particularly in the Cotswolds, where planning regulations are rightly very strict. Scotland has the worst council housing, and away from the industrial regions this is in areas where stone buildings are predominant in their very modest vernacular styles.

Stone deteriorates in many ways. Careless quarrying may have caused tiny fractures even before the material was used in building; it may have been laid against its natural bedding; it may have been used in conjunction with an unsuitable 'bed-mate', that is, a magnesian limestone could gradually impregnate a neighbouring limestone or sandstone with magnesium sulphate, thus weakening it. But most stone decay is caused through atmospheric pollution and weathering, or the effects of plant growth. Chalk and the softer limestones are the most vulnerable; granite, slate, flint and gritstone the most impervious and therefore longest lasting. Cleaning stonework can help to arrest the processes of decay as well as restoring its appearance to something like the original. Generally speaking, this is a specialised task, since care is needed to avoid removing any part of the surface skin, and to avoid damaging the natural patina which age has added to the masonry. Technical advice about cleaning of stonework may be obtained through the Department of the Environment, and from the Building Research Station at Garstone, near Watford.

When I look closely at the stone walls of my house, or the walls of houses in the village, I can distinguish by their colour variation thin lines of strata in the stone. Down the hill some field walls are of limestone, rich in tiny marine fossils, additional proof that all the local stone was once laid down as sediments in ancient seas. Even where they are built of chalk, stone of such villages is of primeval origins, while those of granite and slates is older still. In this respect it can be claimed that stone villages are built from the oldest materials available, and I can say, with a degree of truth, that my house and my village are about 300 million years old. Perhaps it is the sub-conscious realisation of this factor that helps to create the unique sense of place which is the proud characteristic of stone villages.

2
Lure of the Limestone

The great belt of limestone which touches many counties between Dorset and North Yorkshire can realistically be called the architectural backbone of England. Yet to describe it as a belt over-simplifies the picture, implying as it does a uniformity. In fact, the stone varies in colour and texture from one area to another, often from one quarry to another, yet sharing the common ancestry of having been laid down in warm, shallow waters of seas far distant in time. Geologists call it the Jurassic period and it happened between 140 and 195 million years ago when corals, sea-lilies and other plants and organisms lived in the blue seas which then covered the greater part of England. Falling, when dead, like a suspended powder to the sea-bed, they formed the layers of rock which we now call the Inferior Oolite and Great Oolite, named from the tiny, naturally cemented, spherical specks resembling herring-roe, or even mini frog-spawn. As the waters subsequently receded, and the uneven sea-bed became an undulating land surface, these Jurassic Limestones dried out and, smoothed by wind and weather, now form the gracious uplands of England, with long, sweeping ridges, escarpments, and gentle valleys rarely blighted by industry. For twenty centuries the stone – grey, buff, cream, honey-coloured, golden – has been mined or quarried, sawn, carved and decorated by generations of quarrymen, masons, builders and craftsmen who have raised and created some of the most beautiful buildings ever made.

Both oolites are soft when quarried, relatively easy to work into fine detail, and harden on exposure to the air. They have another quality, less easy to define, but best described as a faithfulness. Although they are used to some extent outside their geological boundaries, especially for major buildings like cathedrals and churches, they do not admit intruders – or did not, until modern times allowed peculiar hybrids to infiltrate. Thus, the oolite invades but is rarely invaded. The edge of the stone forms a very uneven boundary in its irregular march north-eastwards across the country, so that its alien neighbours occasionally intrude its flanks, but houses and villages on the oolite are true to it, and have come from it. The limestone itself rose from beneath the sea, so it seems appropriate to start this survey on the Dorset coast where it still does just that.

The Isle of Portland – Hardy's 'Isle of Slingers, carved by Time out of a single stone' – is Dorset's final peninsular thrust of the Jurassic Limestone. No

Weston, Isle of Portland. Houses grow from a stone landscape. Large blocks of masonry in wall. Attic windows are disastrous, though

trees fret its bleak skyline, and its windswept plateau is pockmarked with old quarries. Cyclopean blocks of stone frame views of austere villages. In Easton no amount of colour-wash can disguise the huge size of stones in house walls, and great slabs make crude but effective porches. A single thatched roof is a rare accent in a sea of Welsh slate.

In no way can Portland's landscape or villages be called beautiful, yet Portland stone has produced some of England's finest buildings. St George, Reforme, now redundant, is probably Dorset's most impressive eighteenth-century church, surrounded by waving grasses and wild flowers in a churchyard where hundreds of headstones commemorate quarrymen, masons and sailors. Lichen and trailing greenery warm embellishments and good lettering in Portland's pale grey stone. Westwards is the great swathe of Chesil Beach; eastwards, beyond Weymouth, is the county's other non-island, Purbeck.

From Swanage to Corfe Castle former quarry villages seem to grow from stony fields and hawthorns edge old workings. Langton Matravers is grey and unostentatious, while Worth Matravers, pleasant but over-prettified, is no longer the home of old quarrymen and stonemasons. Farther west along the Purbeck limestone ridge, G. E. Street's stately church of 1880 – arguably his best work – dominates the neat estate village of Kingston. Stone houses comfortably border a raised pavement of stone flags, with a prominent pump, overlooked by latticed windows. By a pub on the corner the road from Swanage turns its back on the sea and heads for Corfe Castle.

The village is named after the castle whose proud, gaunt ruins stand sentinel at the only cleft in the chalk rampart which separates the Isle of Purbeck from the heathlands stretching northwards to Wareham. The castle, hill-poised above houses of grey stone, gave purpose and protection to the medieval village, but brings people and popularity to its successor. From church and market place two roads diverge southwards. East Street has the through traffic, West Street the advantage of finishing among fields. The view from the raised churchyard reveals its harmonies. Sunlight slants across stone-slate roofs, heavy and sagging into gentle hollows subtle with shade; stone walls, gables, dormers and chimneys give point and counterpoint; window-frames and lintels create white accents of rhythm, and the street's gentle curves reveal new perspectives. Best of all is the northward view – castle, church and cottages in a unified symphony of grey Purbeck stone.

Cream, buff or pale gold when first quarried, the weathered grey of Purbeck stone is revealed in villages between Swanage and Dorchester. Westwards from Hardy's Casterbridge, and also from Weymouth, the oolite is encountered. In

Corfe Castle

Corfe Castle, Dorset. Complete unity in Purbeck stone – rubble walls, heavy stone-slate roofs with gabled or eyebrow dormers. Note the wooden lintels

Burton Bradstock, Dorset. Colour-wash lightens the walls of rubble limestone without completely hiding the texture

banded cliffs at Burton Bradstock it meets the Channel shore, by the hilt end of Chesil's curving blade of pebbles. The road through Burton Bradstock throws off cross lanes like little limbs, lined with rows of thatched cottages. From narrow plots, flowers creep up colour-washed walls almost to eaves-shaded upper windows. Wooden lintels are sometimes black-painted, doors and window-frames white or blue. Near the school and village hall a small, intimate green provides the one focal point in Burton Bradstock's informal beauty.

Abbotsbury, to the east, is assertively linear. Continuous rows of cottages, mainly thatched and faintly formal above raised pavements, converge at a widening of Market Street, once a busy focus in Abbotsbury's important days before the Dissolution of the Monasteries. Stone from old quarries at Portesham nearby was used for the cottages and former abbey buildings, as it was in Portesham itself, where tiny gardens line narrow lanes and a clear stream ripples past the church. Little Bredy is similarly water-blessed, below the Dorset chalk.

The Jurassic Limestone, however, writhes northwards in a narrow belt, broadening and swelling beyond Beaminster and then turning eastwards towards Sherborne. High-hedged, sometimes tree-tunnelled lanes, lead to secretive stone villages beneath sheltering, flat-topped hills where wind-waved grasses fringe ramparts of Iron Age forts. Dorset's villages catch echoes of a past far more apparent than anywhere else in the stone belt. The landscape ordains other differences. Enclosing hills squeeze villages into huddles, as at Stoke Abbot, where short rows of cottages front the road leading past the church, and a spring leaps out from a ferny bank. Walls have different sized stones, often unusually large, with small shaped ones in lintels above doors and neat casement windows.

Eggardon Hill casts a protective spur towards Powerstock, where buff-grey cottages, smiling gardens and orchards langour by the grey stone church, and lichened headstones lean beyond the churchyard wall. Symondsbury enjoys the intimacy of tall trees, and, as in other villages of the Dorset stone, cottages are graced with gardens, often raised above road level behind high retaining walls. Thatched roofs, eyebrowed dormers gay with rose or clematis, and garlanded porches, compensate for the cooler colours of this stone compared to the warmer tones of Cotswold country.

John Betjeman praised the euphony of Dorset place-names, but not even Ryme Intrinseca matches its music. Yetminster, next door, its stone more golden than most, has houses with mullioned and drip-stoned windows, and some doorways with four-centred heads. The main street is as good as any in Dorset for showing the range of vernacular buildings in stone spanning 150 years up to about 1730. To the south-west, across the main Yeovil road, and approached along a flowery, ferny lane, Melbury Osmond benefits from its hillside situation. Seventeenth- and eighteenth-century houses, some thatched, some slated, informally line both sides of the street which descends to a ford. Seen from the stream at the bottom, where the road ends, the village grows up the hill towards its church, a sequence of walls, gables, roofs, warm-tinged in afternoon sunlight.

Sherborne has kept faith with its abbey, its past, and its environment, where the northward progress of the oolite is marked by a range of gentle green hills. Sandford Orcas, Corton Denham and South Cadbury nestle beneath the ridges, their stone more golden than the greyer Holton, Bratton Seymour and Charlton Horethorne to the east. Beyond Bruton the limestone is deflected eastwards by the Mendips of Somerset, while on the skyline Alfred's Tower announces the western limit of Wiltshire's chalklands. Near Shepton Mallet Doulting's famous quarries provided stone for Glastonbury Abbey and Wells Cathedral, but the village disappoints. Even its great fifteenth-century Abbey Barn, with massive gabled porches, suffers the indignity of corrugated iron. Aldhelm, first Bishop of Sherborne, and one of the great scholar-saints of Wessex, died at Doulting in 709. His funeral procession to Malmesbury in north Wiltshire must have followed the limestone – a stone he himself chose for his wonderful Saxon church at Bradford-on-Avon – along the Somerset–Wiltshire border.

About 15 miles (24km) east of Bruton, Purbeck stone makes an unexpected reappearance. Surrounded by chalk downland near the head of the Nadder valley, quarries at Tisbury and Chilmark yielded almost identical oolites, fine grained and creamy-white when fresh, weathering grey, and occasionally green-tinged with glauconite. Chilmark provided stone for Salisbury Cathedral and Romsey Abbey as well as local mansions, while villages along the Nadder have used it extensively. Although Tisbury has suffered from too much Victorian and more recent brick, Place Farm nearby is the remarkable survival of a fifteenth-century grange of Shaftesbury Abbey, with farm buildings, gatehouse, and enormous tithe-barn whose roof has probably the largest area of thatch in the country. Dressed blocks of local stone indicate an early prosperity.

Chilmark itself shows the prodigal use of stone to be expected in a former quarry village, with house walls characterised by large blocks, roughly squared, of different sizes. Many windows are stone-mullioned, roofs steeply pitched and thatched, and a clear stream chuckles along one side of the main street. Chilmark is a summer-evening village, when sunlight glances across textured walls, warm toned with pink-brown lichen.

Fovant, Dinton, Barford St Martin and the Teffonts all show Chilmark stone used in the calm setting of a chalk-stream valley. Embowered in trees, Teffont Magna and Teffont Evias share a sparkling stream which swells the Nadder. Small stone bridges lead to gracious houses in walled, well-kept gardens, and a turreted seventeenth-century manor-house, now converted into flats, has a tiny church at a corner of its lawns. West of Chilmark, woodlands

Chilmark, Wiltshire. Grey limestone of seventeenth-century houses in a famous quarry village

and lakes of the Fonthill estates are a more lasting asset to the landscape than was Beckford's Gothic fantasy, Fonthill Abbey, whose soaring tower collapsed in 1825, after being too hurriedly built a few years earlier. Its Chilmark stone was not to blame, but the ruins were a useful quarry, the stones finding their way to houses at Fonthill Gifford and Fonthill Bishop.

East Knoyle lies beneath sheltering beechwoods at the western limit of Wiltshire's wedge of oolite. Christopher Wren, son of the rector, was born here in 1632, and it would be satisfying to reflect that the local stone, seen in church and village houses of his boyhood – as it is today – may have influenced him in later years when he chose its Portland cousin for his great London churches. Whereas East Knoyle and the neighbouring villages of Chilmark stone are, as it were, intruders in chalk country, villages on the limestone's march along the Wiltshire–Somerset border to Bath are of the limestone, and integral to it, although the stone never dominates, as occurs in the Cotswolds, because it is less commonly used for roofs. Tiles, pantiles, thatch and Welsh slate break the stronghold of stone, adding their own contrasts of colour and texture.

Mells is a gem, a scatter of stone houses in the wooded Wadbury valley west of Frome, with a couple of tiny greens. In a county of noble church towers it has one of the grandest, mightily buttressed and proud with pinnacles. Very humble, however, is the double row of cottages in New Street by the

Mells, Somerset. New Street, one of England's oldest streets. New in 1470 when Abbot Selwood planned a small town, this is all that was completed

churchyard entrance. New in 1470, the only completed part of Abbot Selwood's plan to create a small town, it is one of England's oldest surviving streets, still displaying its Tudor origins, but with seventeenth-century details, especially windows, superimposed.

Nearby, at the eastern end of Mendip, Nunney has all the right ingredients for a fairy-tale village – moated medieval castle with round corner-towers, grey stone, red-tiled houses by a clear, rippling stream, an elegant manor-house, a church on the hill, and a pub whose signboard spans the village street. Planned or just organic, the result could scarcely be improved. Even the busy A361 is kept at a respectful distance.

In north Somerset and west Wiltshire villages proliferate, reflecting five centuries of wool and cloth prosperity. Lullington, with its large green, Beckington, Norton St Philip and Hinton Charterhouse all have houses of grey stone, some gabled, but generally without ostentation. Stone mullions are few, and a major building focuses attention. At Norton St Philip, the George Inn, built by the priors of Hinton as a wool-staple, but used as a tavern for five hundred years, is a blend of stone with half-timbering, a rarity on this Jurassic journey. The northwards-flowing River Frome provided water-power for wool-cloth mills, now vanished or derelict and silent, and weavers' cottages abound in small villages like Tellisford, whose narrow packhorse bridge saw its busy days two or three centuries ago. Westwood was the home of the great clothier family of Horton, and the land around is honeycombed with tunnels of old stone mines. Freshford, where the Frome joins the Avon among fields, wooded hills and old mills, reflects the fashionable influences of nearby Bath in a spectrum of styles in stone, with stone slates being used for roofs. Limpley Stoke is attractively terraced on the steep western hillside above the Avon, whose north-flowing course here in its most scenic section is enhanced by Rennie's graceful Dundas Aqueduct carrying the Kennet & Avon Canal across the valley.

Steep-sided valleys among the crumpled green hills south of Bath help village identities to survive in surroundings remarkably rural so close to a city. Physical factors have imposed their own limits on village spread. South Stoke, 3 miles (4.8km) from the city's heart, retains not only a distinctive village character but a magnificent fifteenth-century barn with a dovecote in its gabled porch, honeyed stone buildings of Manor Farm, and a Packhorse Inn which would be at home in any Cotswold village. Wellow's proud church surveys a village street of good stone houses; Combe Hay Manor is a Georgian gem, with a church in a corner of its parkland, and stone cottages tucked away along secretive lanes. It is hard to imagine the impact here of the Somerset Coal Canal, planned to follow the winding valley of the Cam Brook, linking the Somerset coalfield with the Kennet & Avon at Dundas. William Smith was its surveyor, and lived in a stone cottage at Tucking Mill between Midford and Monkton Combe towards the end of the eighteenth century. During his work for the canal company, he evolved, through fossil identification, the idea of sequence in rock strata, a new concept in geology which earned him the title 'Father of English Geology'.

Between Bradford-on-Avon and Bath the Avon has cut a valley through the limestone. Northwards, the landscape becomes increasingly Cotswold in character. A Pleiades of villages and manors – Monkton Farleigh, South Wraxall, Atworth, Neston – are curtain-raisers in silvery-grey limestone for the subsequent delights of true Cotswold style, and are none the worse for being away from main roads. Bath stone has been mined or quarried from beds in the hills around Bath since Roman times. A fine-grained freestone, pale honey to aggressive yellow in colour, it gained fashionable status during the eighteenth and nineteenth centuries, and in the area around Box, Corsham and Monkton Farleigh over 60 miles (96km) of tunnels penetrate underground beds. In only one, near Corsham, is Bath stone still being worked, although recent attempts have been made to reopen a small mine near Limpley Stoke.

Cotswold is both a region and a building style. From Dyrham Park to Dover's Hill, 50 crow-flying miles (80km) embrace the Cotswold's western scarp. The A46 climbs from Bath to the beginning of the edge, and Meon Hill, beyond Chipping Campden, is its *coup de grâce*. From its highest points on the west, just topping 1,000ft (300m) the Cotswold plateau slopes gently south and east with first the Avon, then the Thames and finally the Cherwell forming natural boundaries. Other streams and rivers drain the limestone uplands – Frome, Coln, Leach, Windrush, Evenlode – village-makers all, providing water for the needs of man and beast, for washing wool and cloth, for powering mills.

Scratch a Cotswold sheepwalk and you will find the stone beneath, always amenable to masons' skills. Golden stone transmutes to golden fleece. For centuries sheep grazed sweet pastures on these broad-breasted hills. Their wool brought wealth, first to monasteries, later to merchants. Fortunes went into the building of abbeys, splendid churches, fine houses, and, after the Dissolution of the Monasteries, smaller houses. Masons of the seventeenth and eighteenth centuries used the same stone, the same tools, crafts and skills as their forebears who worked on medieval monasteries and the great Perpendicular wool churches. As Freda Derrick described it, 'On the Cotswolds the stone is in the blood'.

Although its finest flowering was between about 1570 and 1720, and it continued to flourish long afterwards, the Cotswold vernacular was inspired by the Elizabethan period successfully absorbing classical mannerisms as well as Victorian and later Gothic revivals. Details changed, but proportions remained the same, as did the stone, and therefore the unity in the overall appearance of a house, barn, cottage, terrace or street. It is the stone which holds the secret, identified by J. B. Priestley fifty years ago: 'Even when the sun is obscured and the light is cold . . . these walls are still faintly warm and luminous as if they knew the trick of keeping the lost sunlight of centuries glimmering about them.'

Another factor is involved. Wherever shines the sun there also falls a shadow. If Cotswold stone possesses its own ambient brilliance in sunlight, shadows cast by gabled dormers, chimneys, overlapping roof-slates, porches, dripstones, even the tiny ooliths themselves, create contrast and counterpoint. Yet, with a converse quirkiness, this same stone can assume a cloak of near-invisibility. Its universal use for walls, roofs, barns and farm buildings means that on sunless, shadowless days farm groups, hamlets, even whole villages seen from a distance, are formless smudges on the scene. But when sunlight gleams on them they seem to appear from the landscape as though they were manifestations of the earth itself – which, of course, they are.

Painswick, Burford and Chipping Campden are roughly at the points of a triangle which encloses the area of best Cotswold stones, in a countryside of gentle cadences. The three places are themselves large villages with the regional importance of small wool towns. Each shows the full spectrum of Cotswold style in its different way. Hill-perched Painswick is compact, its small town houses of creamy-grey stone grouped in narrow streets or small enclaves. Every corner reveals a new scene of gables, windows, porches, or a glimpse of a distant hillside. The inward view is always to the church, in England's most beautiful churchyard graced with exuberantly carved memorials to generations of clothiers, and shadowed by ninety-nine yews.

Burford

Burford's present is as busy as its past, the buildings which line its handsome main street showing a fine miscellany of styles with a rich diversity in doorways, hoods and porches. Groupings near the bottom of the street, where the Windrush washes Burford's feet, seem almost to be a final flourish of Cotswold, and in its crowded churchyard bale-tombs of seventeenth-century clothiers emphasise earlier prosperity.

Five centuries of the instinctive genius of Cotswold masons harmonise in the unity of Chipping Campden's gently curving, graceful street. Warm, grey-gold stone modulates in changing light, shimmering beneath summer suns, magical by moonlight. Its buildings are a parade of beauty, even if the proudest merchants' houses are now hotels and the smaller ones occupied by Midlands' commuters and fairly affluent pensioners. Like any other good street it has a focal point, the seventeenth-century market hall. A feature of Campden's street is the number of flat, ground-floor bay-windows, often combined with the front door under a single, stone-slated roof, echoing in a minor key the pattern of the main roof, repeating its darker tones and horizontal lines. A number of these bay-windowed cottages were formerly shops. Campden's door-hoods and porches gave local masons a new challenge during the eighteenth century, and nowhere in the Cotswolds is there so rich a collection.

A hillside of soft fruit bushes, orchards with sheep and goats, embower Ebrington, two miles east of Campden, with a softness unusual in Cotswold country. Cottages of glowing stone stand above grassy banks rich in summer with ferns and foxgloves; stone steps are informally scattered around, and on the small green oak trees give friendly shade to seats, while farms and rickyards facing the village street balance the rosy image with reality.

Broadway's High Street, lined with perfect Cotswold cottages and houses, honey-coloured, gabled, dormered and bay-windowed, climbs gently up a hill from an informal green. Occasional half-timbering and thatch soften the texture and the tone without diminishing the ethos. Broadway's courtesan charm undoubtedly brings it the pleasures and pains of popularity, like those experienced by Castle Combe, podded in the sheltered By Brook valley at Cotswold's southern margin. Spanned by its low-arched stone bridge, a stream touches the end of the village, where textured cottages lead to a small square, with a medieval market cross its focus, symbol of fifteenth-century industrial prosperity. Small, compact, intimate, colourful, Castle Combe is the archetypal Cotswold village.

Water contributes to the character of many other villages making them summer honeypots. Clear glides the trout-rich Coln beneath the bridges at Bibury. Across a meadow the cottage windows of Arlington Row gaze from their shadows, their gables glanced by sunlight. Formerly a fourteenth-century barn or sheep-house, the building was converted in the seventeenth century to house weavers working at Arlington Mill. Bibury churchyard, like

Ebrington

others around Burford, contains a few bale-tombs, easily identified by the decorative 'bolsters' on their tops, commemorating seventeenth-century clothiers. Nearby is Ablington, setting of *A Cotswold Village*, written in 1898 by its young squire Arthur Gibbs, a book which was instrumental in creating a greater awareness of this region as a unique part of England. A picture of the Cotswolds a generation later is given us by Laurie Lee who lived as a young boy in Slad, near Painswick, in the decade after World War I. His *Cider with Rosie* recalled with affectionate detail those distant days when, with his mother and seven brothers and sisters, he lived in part of a Cotswold house with 'hand-carved windows, golden surfaces, moss-flaked tiles, and walls so thick they kept a damp chill inside whatever the season or weather'.

In the valley of the Leach the little river separates Eastleach Martin and Eastleach Turville. River and road run through water meadows, stone walls

35

parallel the river, and Keble's Bridge of stone slabs is a convenient crossing between two churches; but the terraced cottages of Turville keep their distance from the stream. If this is rural Cotswold, Bourton-on-the-Water is very nearly urban, with the Windrush gliding, controlled and contrived, beneath neat little eighteenth-century bridges, with lawns and willows overtly formal a setting for Cotswold houses of average quality. Upstream, the Slaughters are happier in more rural surroundings. Trim cottages at Lower Slaughter draw away from the water, making space for stretches of green, summer-shaded with ash, beech and lime, in colour and shape a foil for mellowed masonry. Small stone bridges complete the harmony, but a nineteenth-century cornmill with waterwheel intrudes as the only brick structure in the village, and now serves as shop, bakery and post office. Some modern housing continues the traditional style, but at Upper Slaughter no new houses have been added since 1904, although cottages in the small square were remodelled soon afterwards by Lutyens.

At Bledington, near Stow-on-the-Wold, a stream glides through the centre of a generous green, and garden walls are of vertical slabs of grey stone – an idiom also used at Filkins, near Lechlade, a compact village with high walls garlanded with flowers given by villagers. Although many Cotswold villages have small greens, few of these are dominant features. At Little Barrington the head waters of a small stream have channelled a course down the centre of a rough green, backed by a terrace of eighteenth-century cottages rustically unostentatious.

Valleys may make for more prosperous villages, but those of upland Cotswold between the Fosse Way and the western edge seem more rooted in the soil. There the Cotswold farms and their associated buildings predominate in the scene, even more than church and manor-house. Hampnett, Turkdean, Hasleton, Cold Aston, Notgrove, Naunton, Cutsdean and Snowshill are all reached by very minor roads between splendid Cotswold walls. Villages make up in quiet, rural charm for what they may lack in architectural exuberance. Below the escarpment, however, south of Broadway, Stanton exudes Cotswold perfection and apparent authenticity. Half-climbing a wooded slope facing Bredon Hill, its gabled cottages, with window glass set directly into grooved stone, are of the great period 1570–1650, but their present appearance owes much to the rebuilding work carried out during the 1920s by skilled craftsmen under the direction of the architect-squire Sir Philip Scott.

The unity of many Cotswold villages is the result of their being squirearchal. A single person, usually the lord of the manor, has owned and controlled the village, its appearance and economy. On the southern edge Great Barrington is very much a ducal creation, while in the Coln valley Hatherop and Coln St Aldwyns display similar estate-village characteristics, even to the extent of insisting that a modern bus shelter is constructed in correct Cotswold style. Sherborne, set in open parkland by the Sherborne

Snowshill, Gloucestershire. The Cotswold idiom at its simplest. It could be 1600 or 1800 – the materials, shapes and proportions are the same

brook which feeds the Windrush, has casual groups of estate cottages, and one detached, dormered house incorporating arches of late Norman masonry.

Windrush's hillside situation below the ridge which carries the A40 contributes to its fine clusters of roofs, gables, chimneys and dormers, while across the Oxfordshire border to the east, Taynton's quiet, winding street reveals a series of Cotswold cameos, of steep, deep-toned roofs, mullioned windows with drip-moulds, and grey-buff walls. Stone from quarries at Taynton, Barrington and Windrush was worked by generations of famous masons, Kempsters and Strongs among them, whose skill took them to work on Oxford colleges, Blenheim Palace and St Paul's Cathedral itself. Near the Fox Inn between the Barringtons is a spot called The Wharf, where local stone was loaded on to barges and floated down the Windrush to the Thames.

Industry has not tarnished the face of Cotswold. Blockley, east of Campden, experienced about 150 years of silk manufacture from soon after 1700. On a steep valley side above the Knee Brook, terraces of cottages were built on narrow shelves at different levels, paralleled by lines of low mills, so that the village is a strata of buildings. The mills have become country houses, the cottages happily occupied. Alleys lead up and down steep clefts, and even High Street is suitable really only for pedestrians. Just as situation and social history have given Blockley a distinctive character, so, too, has Chalford acquired its unique aspect. On Cotswold's southern edge, the River Frome takes a westwards course to the Avon. Beechwoods clothe the hillsides, presenting in autumn a burnished backcloth to merit its sobriquet, Golden Valley. Chalford's cottages cling in short rows along and up the northern slopes, so that walls and windows of one row appear to grow from roofs and chimneys of the group beneath. The scene may be more industrial, evoking the early years of last century, with many-windowed mills and even an old canal, but the style is still Cotswold, the river and its valley making no distinction between one type of Cotswold country and another.

The Evenlode, however, is different. Pre-eminently it is the river which divides the Gloucestershire Cotswolds from Oxfordshire, and for a couple of miles north of Bledington forms a wriggling county boundary. Eastwards is the landscape of the Oxford Clays, and although stone villages abound, with angles and corners and textures so very nearly Cotswold, the valley settings, wooded hillsides and wind-washed western wolds have been left behind, and the landscape has lost its secret places.

Kingham is a widely scattered village with good seventeenth-century houses near the church, a wide green at the opposite end, and, in West Street, the rare survival of a thirteenth-century stone chimney above Manor Cottages. Nearby is Adlestrop, where, on a hot summer afternoon just before World War I, Edward Thomas captured a perfect moment from a station name-board, and 'heard all the birds of Oxfordshire and Gloucestershire'. The name-board is now in the village bus shelter, and the curving street still has golden-stone cottages, gardens full of flowers, and a thatched post office and telephone box. Nearby, mid-Victorian estate houses by the gates of Daylesford Park are resplendent with groups of stone chimneys and decorated gables.

Cornwell is contrived but charming, the creation of Clough Williams-Ellis in the 1930s. Stone cottages roofed with Stonesfield slates, neatly terraced and grouped on a hillside by a stream canalised into a pool, are focused on a small formal green bordered by stone walls. Finials flourish, white paint picks out glazing bars of Queen Anne-style windows, and cobbles discourage cars in this Portmeirionised piece of Cotswold. The grey-buff limestone continues eastwards, touching the ghostly reminders of Wychwood's ancient forest. On a ridge between the Evenlode and Glyme poignancy pervades the grass-grown quarries which for centuries yielded the beautiful Stonesfield slates that adorn thousands of Cotswold roofs.

Stone villages are regularly dispersed north-eastwards from Bicester in a pleasant but undramatic landscape broken by small winding rivers. Farms and their associated buildings underline Marsh Gibbon's rural nature, and black-painted wooden lintels over windows are an indication that the Cotswold idiom has been left far behind. Thornborough, near Buckingham, has a long, spacious green with trees, a duck-happy stream, houses of coarse

Wadenhoe, Northamptonshire. Rubble-stone and thatch, in the Nene valley

rubble-stone, some thatched, some tiled. North of Stony Stratford and Watling Street, Castlethorpe's stone cottages surround a square green, with church in one corner, while Hanslope's soaring spire is a foretaste of splendours yet to come. Hanslope village, with cottages of rough, buff-coloured stone, some thatch, some tile, tiny dormers, wooden lintels, loosely grouped round a pleasant square, is as good as any in this northern corner of Buckinghamshire.

But it is where the oolite moves to a northward course that the stone produces the finest villages and domestic buildings outside the Cotswolds. Within 25 miles (40km) of Stamford famous quarries abound, yielding fine-grained limestones, grey, creamy-white, buff and pale yellow, all capable of taking a fine ashlared finish. North of Kettering and Thrapston, where patches of woodland survive in the area formerly covered by Rockingham

Forest, bounded roughly by the Welland and Nene, villages are almost wholly of stone. In a county where steeples pierce the skyline Titchmarsh's proud tower seems to have escaped from Somerset, while at Wadenhoe, across the Nene, the village has escaped from its church, solitary on a grassy knoll. Farms and thatched cottages line the main street, another group guards a small green, and pantiles replace some thatch. Timeless and shopless, Wadenhoe slumbers. Aldwincle, nearby, curves gracefully past a redundant church, opposite the thatched rectory where Dryden was born, and a few miles down-river Barnwell, sheltered by mature limes and dipping willows and blessed by a stream flowing down the green centre of the village, has Montagu memories and a royal presence. Cottages of buff-grey stone, thatched or tiled, and crowned with clusters of elegant chimneys, curve in a semi-circle near the church. Gable finials suggest a more Cotswold exuberance than the county normally displays, while Barnwell Castle's massive bastions create a dramatic full-stop to the village.

Some miles to the west, Geddington, too, has royal associations. The three entries to the village meet in a small square, graced by the best preserved of the three surviving Eleanor Crosses erected by Edward I to the memory of his adored queen who died in 1290. Statues, niches, pinnacles, flowers, scarcely ever restored, bear witness to the enduring qualities of the Weldon stone from

Duddington

40

which they were carved almost seven centuries ago. Stone houses, many with thatch, line the square and village streets, and the sturdy arches of Geddington's medieval bridge across the reed-fringed Ise, link the main part of the village, via Queen Street, to its modern expansion along the busy A13.

A map entitled 'Kettering and Corby' may not seem very encouraging to the seeker of stone villages, but, like so many Ordnance Survey sheets in the 1:50,000 Series, it offers its own secrets and rewards. Regularly sited 2–3 miles (3.2–4.8km) apart, they are a succession of quiet places, unpretentious and unsophisticated. Grafton Underwood has houses reached by stone bridges across the stream; Cotterstock, Woodnewton, Apethorpe and King's Cliffe are full of good grey stone houses roofed with Collyweston slates. Bridge Street here has a fine array of almshouses, schools, and William Law's Library of about 1700 bears an inscription above its door, 'Books of piety are here lent to any persons of this or ye neighbouring towns'.

To the west, Barrowden's grey stone cottages trail down a hill to the Welland, with the distant green landscape glimpsed through gaps between cottages; Duddington, with a view of roofs from the top of the street, sun-kissed cottage groups, and a fine mill by the river; and Collyweston itself, which produced the autumn-brown slates for thousands of roofs across these eastern Midlands. Its broad sloping High Street below the church, with

seventeenth-century yeomen's houses on the north and artisans' terraces opposite, reveals the rich rhythm of roofs and perky little dormers, two-storey stone bays, and the shimmering vale beyond. Across the Welland is Ketton, whose famous quarries have for four centuries yielded a noble, slightly granular oolite, mainly buff-yellow but occasionally pink-tinged. Cottage groups and individual houses near the church glow in evening light, and handsome clustered chimneys fret the skyline. Datestones add distinction, and finely carved headstones line the churchyard path above a sunken roadway. Indeed, the 22 miles (35km) of the Welland valley from Market Harborough to Stamford reveals from its hillside roads a succession of fine broad views of rich farmlands, quiet meadows, and stone-built villages culminating with the crescendo charms of Easton on the Hill. Throughout is the inescapable fact that almost all the best houses and cottages in every village date from the seventeenth and eighteenth centuries, the mullioned windows, bayed and gabled, or flush with walls but capped by hood-mouldings characteristic of early Stuart times, all declaring a period of high rural prosperity throughout these Midland counties.

Eastwards, the limestone gradually surrenders itself to the fenland peat, with Ermine Street a rough boundary to the use of stone in village building. Helpston's grey-stone houses around its green probably show a far more prosperous appearance now than when John Clare, the peasant-poet, lived in a small thatched cottage early last century. He discovered as much beauty in overgrown stone quarries nearby as other poets found among high hills. Perhaps they may have been at Barnack, whose famous ragstone quarries were, in the Middle Ages, among the most extensively worked in the country. Grass-covered hummocks now mark the area of long-abandoned quarries, designated as the 'Hills and Hollows' National Nature Reserve.

Stone imparts to Barnack village a unity otherwise denied by a straggling layout. As with other villages in the Stamford region of fine-quality limestones, colours are muted – creamy-buffs, honey and warm greys – well-coursed in house walls, with oak lintels, steeply pitched roofs of Collyweston slates, and mullioned windows without the dripstone mouldings of Gloucestershire vernacular. Gardens in Greatford, across the Lincolnshire border, are adorned with stone embellishments – coronets, mushrooms, obelisks and elephants – a 1930s whimsy of one Major Fitzwilliam adding a happy craziness to a village whose appeal arises also from very good groupings – barns and stables, estate cottages, church and manor-house.

(opposite)

Collyweston, Northamptonshire. Note the dressed stone used for window-dressings and gables. The roof of Collyweston slates was new *c*1960

Ketton, Leicestershire. A large quarry village with an unusually wide range of houses, artisans' to squires', and fine headstones in the churchyard

Easton on the Hill

To the west, Ryhall's neat stone cottages cluster round a small square graced with a central maple tree, while Belmesthorpe's single street of stone includes a noble barn, a dovecote and dormer-windowed houses. Tickencote enjoys a cul-de-sac situation just off the A1, its houses of Ketton stone, thatched or slated, look westwards beyond a sumptuous church to mature parkland and Empingham Reservoir in the distance. In this former Rutland countryside where pasture alternates with parkland, villages hide from view. Exton has sycamores in its large, almost circular green, with stone cottages around and along adjoining lanes. None is spectacular, but here and there bands of ironstone in the walls are a reminder of more contrasting stones nearby.

Clipsham's quarries are, perhaps, the most famous of all in the Stamford area, yielding superb freestones and good ragstones carried all over England. The hardest of all the 'Lincolnshire Limestones', and used since medieval times, Clipsham came into its own from the seventeenth century. The quarries are east of the village which is fragmented and disappointing. Nearby, Castle Bytham makes the most of its sloping site, its rubble-stone cottages informally grouped, with some slate but more pantile, interspersed with occasional brick intruders. A pond at the foot of Pinfold Street, a conduit, and a clear stream by Water Lane have their visual credit marred by an untidy green at the top of the village. Corby Glen's market place, with a cross on a high-stepped plinth, is overlooked by stone houses and the Fighting Cocks with its splendidly bloodthirsty sign. Small stone cottages near the church, and a delightful little grammar school of 1673 are sufficiently rewarding to justify a tiny detour from the A151. Sir Isaac Newton's birthplace at Colsterworth (National Trust) is a focus for visitors, attracted by the name rather than the undistinguished architecture of Woolsthorpe Manor. Other stone houses straggle along the main village street on a limestone ridge above the Witham.

Ancaster's creamy-white oolite is particularly fine-grained, but one bed

44

showing iron-staining gives it a yellow-brown colour. The long street-village is disappointing, with only a few houses of real distinction. For a village sitting almost on a quarry it seems an impertinence to use buff-coloured brick for modern bungalows and infilling, even though from a distance they appear to be built of stone. Ermine Street to the north deviates eastwards from the Lincoln 'Edge', that limestone ridge which thins out in its northwards progress, with a distinct scarp to the west, followed by the A607 'Cliff Road'. Along the Edge the limestone resumes, in a muted way, a breadth of line, of spaciousness and harmony with the sky, last felt on the open Cotswolds. In the villages pantiles add colour above rubble walls; lintels and window surrounds are wood. Caythorpe's two-storeyed cottages are warm-toned, plain but pleasant. Fulbeck could, with justification, regard itself as the best of Lincolnshire's limestone villages, where the Hare and Hounds and the post office face across a small green to the church. Stone walls of High Street slope pleasantly down to the Witham valley calling to mind a memory of Melbury Osmond in distant Dorset. Honey-coloured stone catches afternoon sunlight, and finials add a flourish as though to signify that this is almost the final flowering in the northwards journey of the oolite.

But it is North Yorkshire which claims the northern limit of the oolite, as indeed it does of the chalk. Encircling the Vale of Pickering, wholly on its northern side and around Malton on the south, the oolite reappears, identified on the geological map by a lime-green colour representing the only occurrence in England of the Corallian Limestone strata of the oolite formation. This gives rise to the flat-topped 'tabular hills', with their north-facing escarpments along the southern edge of the North Yorkshire Moors, in an east-west line between the Hambleton Hills and the coast near Scarborough. The limestone dips southwards beneath the Vale of Pickering, reappearing as the Howardian

Fulbeck, Lincolnshire. Pale limestone, dressed window surrounds and pantile roofs

Coxwold

Hills. If you drive from Thirsk to Helmsley, once the top of Sutton Bank is reached, you recognise in the broad open landscape with rich brown soils and grey stone walls the characteristic scenery of oolite country. Small local quarries have yielded fine building stones for a succession of villages – Beadlam, Nawton, Wrelton, and especially Appleton-le-Moors, on the north side of the vale; and Langton, Settrington, and the Castle Howard estate villages of Terrington, Bulmer and Coneysthorpe on the south. Only at Hovingham, however, is the oolite still quarried, as a hard, creamy-grey rubble-stone from the upper strata, a cooler-grey freestone below.

Hovingham itself is a large village adjoining the entrance to Hovingham Hall, built wholly of local stone and roofed in pink pantile. A parkland setting, mature trees, generous greens, a chuckling stream, groups and rows of well-proportioned stone houses and cottages, mainly Victorian but interspersed with some eighteenth-century ones, combine in a picture of informal harmony and aesthetic appeal hard to better anywhere in the country. Within a few miles there is a plethora of stone villages, mainly of early nineteenth-century and Victorian rebuilding on the numerous estates, which makes the area around Malton, Pickering and Helmsley so memorable and rewarding.

In name, situation and appearance Coxwold, at the western end of the limestone ridge of the Howardian Hills, recalls its Cotswold cousins at the heart of the Jurassic belt. Its steep main street, bordered by cobbled gutters and grassy banks, is lined with a variety of honey-coloured stone houses along each side. Seventeenth-century almshouses contrast with Victorian cottages, many bearing the initials of the Wombwell family who owned the local estate. Roofs are of stone-slate or pantile, well appreciated in the view of the village from the lychgate by the octagonal-towered church at the top of the hill. Nearby, Colville Hall, the Old Hall and Shandy Hall, the former home of Laurence Sterne, add particular distinction, even though the eccentric curate's house is partly of mellowed brick. Nevertheless, Coxwold seems to me to be an ideal village to bestow benediction on the most gracious stone.

(*opposite top*) Hovingham, North Yorkshire.
Grey-buff limestone and pantile in a fine estate village

3
Along the Lias

The Lias follows the oolite to Lincolnshire and beyond. Rarely as broad, it is a quirky, frivolous neighbour wobbling its way from Celtic Wessex to the Danelaw, always to the west or north-west, but in Northamptonshire breaching the oolite and doubling back on itself. Lias landscapes, especially in the south-west, are more tumbled and restless in form by comparison with the calmer tranquillity of the oolite. A look at its hilltops reveals its character. Cotswold uplands are flat, almost featureless, with the valleys holding the greatest delight. But in west Dorset, it is the Lias which adds excitement to landscapes inland from Bridport to Lyme Regis, forming a fine protective crescent of separate hills round the northern rim of Marshwood Vale.

Similar Liassic mannerisms raise conical tors at Montacute, Glastonbury, and the Dundon hills near Street in Somerset, as well as creating a low ridge from South Cadbury to Bruton. North of Bath the Lias is identified as a raised bench along the foot of the Cotswold scarp, but really makes its presence felt in north Oxfordshire and the southernmost lobe of Warwickshire, where, at Edge Hill, the hard Middle Lias ironstone outcrops in the steep, westward-facing scarp overlooking the Vale of the Red Horse.

Banbury is near the centre of a large block of Lias which throws an appendix southwards along the Cherwell before continuing its fragmented north-easterly course between Daventry and Northampton towards east Leicestershire. The marlstone, as these tawny, iron-impregnated Middle Lias Limestones are called, forms the prominent ridge crowned by Belvoir Castle overlooking the Vale of Belvoir to its west, and through much of its East Midlands course imparts a rich chestnut-brown colour to the fields.

Most Lias landscapes support a rich, more mixed farming than those of Cotswold; field boundaries tend to be hedged rather than walled, and the colours of building stones span a far wider spectrum than those of the oolite. The browns and orange-yellows of Oxfordshire and Northamptonshire which give such a warm appearance to villages are in sharp contrast to the cool greys of the Blue Lias which appear in southern Warwickshire, but far more extensively in south and west Somerset, where the Lower Lias throws off a tangent along the Polden Hills to Bridgwater Bay, and creates conical islands in the Somerset lowlands.

Unlike the tones and textures of the Middle and Upper Lias, whose sandy

Plate 1 Rockingham, Northamptonshire.
Tawny-coloured ironstone, thatch, white
woodwork, trim verges, gay flower borders

Plate 2 Snowshill, Gloucestershire. Hillside
setting enhances the perfect Cotswold idiom of
gables, dormers, roofs, honey-gold walls and
lintels, centred on church and green

content makes them attractive to the welcoming growth of grey-green lichens, the harder Blue Lias acquires no patina with age. Occurring in thin, hard bands between layers of clayey shale, it was quarried in smaller pieces, and, often used with a much darker mortar, imparts a meaner appearance to buildings.

In south Somerset, the Fosse Way keeps close to the Lias. Romans and Saxons quarried Ham Hill stone, and from the Middle Ages until recently it has been used for buildings. Its source on Hamdon Hill, a few miles west of Yeovil, is now a country park, pitted and pockmarked into hills and hollows of old quarry workings superimposed on the far older earthen ramparts of an Iron Age hillfort. From the late sixteenth century onwards, villages all around were rebuilt with this seductively attractive stone.

At the northern foot of Hamdon Hill, the houses of Stoke-sub-Hamdon have well-proportioned gables and mullioned windows, and on the road to West Stoke is the priory, a complex of buildings, including barn and ruined dovecote, surviving from the fourteenth- and fifteenth-century chantry for priests. A mile (1.6km) away, Norton-sub-Hamdon is more intimate, with the added distinction of a rare churchyard dovecote, circular, with a conical roof, all of local stone.

On the other side of the hill, Montacute's handsome houses of Ham stone, lining its main street, reflect its former importance as a borough – or more accurately, as two planned boroughs established about 1100 and 1240 along-side each other, each having its own market. Bishopstone and The Borough represent the two nuclei, but by the sixteenth century Montacute was in decline, and at the century's end Edward Phelips, by then a prosperous Elizabethan lawyer, moved his family home from Montacute's Cluniac priory a few hundred yards northwards to its present site of Montacute House, mellow, welcoming and serene, and a National Trust property since 1931. Much of its appeal lies in the golden colour of its Ham stone used throughout, in gables, oriels, transomed windows, balustrades, statues and gazebos, set against the lush south Somerset landscape. Even in those days it cost an enormous sum, £20,000. Village houses have stone-mullioned windows and mellow red-tiled roofs, among which the fifteenth-century Monk's House is, exceptionally, thatched. Terrace cottages in South Street were weavers' homes in the eighteenth century, when the glove trade prospered.

Over four and a half centuries ago, Leland found this part of Somerset a favoured landscape of pastures and fields enclosed by hedgerows and elms. The trees have gone, but the land and villages still seem to smile at their good fortune. Modern building has extended some villages, but many remain reasonably unblemished, their mullioned cottages almost wholly built of Ham stone. New houses at North Perrott continue the traditional style; older ones are thatched or tiled, with drip-moulds above their windows, yet a mile (1.6km) away at Haselbury Plucknett, wooden lintels and brick dressings are

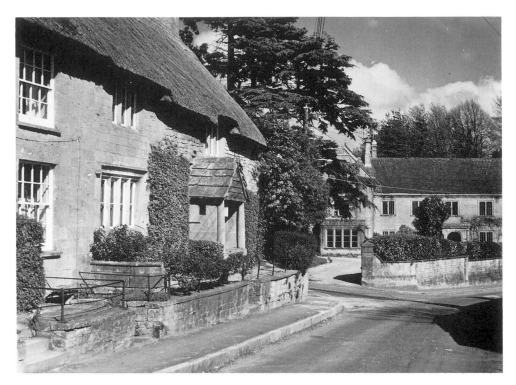

Norton-sub-Hamdon, Somerset. Golden Ham stone, ashlared or rubble, with stone mullions and lintels

Montacute

more evident. Pride of place goes to Hinton St George, most easily approached from the east into a widening High Street whose Poulett Arms marks five centuries of local association with the Poulett family of Hinton House. As so often happens, most of the best houses are on the south side of High Street, denying sun's access to their fronts until summer evenings. Variety of size, shape and age, with the odd white-painted wall, roofs of thatch and pantile, contribute to a lively village scene focused on a fifteenth-century preaching cross at the centre.

North of the Fosse Way, Martock's single street extends for a mile (1.6km) and is unusual in continuing southwards as the main street of smaller settlements of Hurst and Newton before ending in another contiguous village in the same parish, Bower Hinton. Martock itself possesses the dignity of a small town, all of Ham stone. An endowed grammar school of 1661, stone-mullioned with four-centred arched windows, a contemporary manor-house rebuilt last century, a small Georgian arcaded town hall, all add distinction to the place; but Martock's gem is its fourteenth-century Treasurer's House, so named because its rector was Treasurer of Wells Cathedral, and now in the care of the National Trust.

South and west of Yeovil the Lias is only one part of a complex geological jumble, where roads and lanes cut through deep wooded gorges to emerge at villages of honey-gold stone. East Chinnock and West Coker are on the busy A30, but East Coker to the south enjoys a more relaxed existence. Houses and cottages line both sides of the street, with little bridges spanning the stream on the south side. Small gardens gay with flowers supplement the white and blue paint of woodwork against an overall glow of stone and thatch. From a small green the row of Helyar almshouses, founded in 1640, leads to the church, where the great seventeenth-century mariner William Dampier is buried. It was from East Coker, also, that T. S. Eliot's Puritan forebears migrated to New England, and the poet commemorates the village in the second of his 'Four Quartets', written in 1940. Twenty-five years later his ashes were buried here, and the intervening decades have seen little to change:

> Where you lean against a bank while a van passes,
> And the deep lane insists on the direction
> Into the village . . .

East of Yeovil, and beyond the River Yeo which, for a while, separates Somerset from Dorset, the Lias continues its erratic course, forming individual hills by the Comptons, Trent, Sandford Orcas and Corton Denham, to the Cadburys. Trent is a gem, though scarcely large enough to have a single street. Stone throughout, with never a discordant note, from the fifteenth-century chantry by the church – itself one of Dorset's best, and rare in having a spire – Dairy Farm, Church Farm, manor-house all contemporary with it, with later additions and changes. Rectory, Manor Farm and Flamberts represent the

East Coker, Somerset. Rubble Ham stone, thatch and wooden lintels

sixteenth and seventeenth centuries, while the Turner Almshouses of 1846 continue the Tudor tradition. To the north-east, Sandford Orcas straggles along a sketchy stream in a sheltered valley between Windmill Hill and Holway Hill. Houses and cottages of Ham stone, stone-mullioned, some thatched, lead the winding way to church and sixteenth-century manor-house, aloof at the northern end of the village: an early Tudor group above high walls of grey-lichened stone.

To the north and north-west of Yeovil, Somerset's belt of Blue Lias curves round in a broad V-shaped swathe, its open arms to the west, and its eastern apex near Castle Cary. Whole villages are built of it, especially around Somerton and Langport and along the Polden Hills, but few are distinguished. The Dundons, south of Street, have a number of thatched cottages, but pantiles are more common in most villages. High Ham, overlooking Sedgemoor, is nicely grouped around an enclosed green, and sandstone dressings around doors and windows add warmth to the creamy-grey stone.

Butleigh, Baltonsborough, Keinton Mandeville and Pilton are characteristic Somerset villages on the edge of the Somerset 'moors', but probably the best of the Blue Lias villages is Queen Camel, a mile (1.6km) south of the A303 near Sparkford. Edward I gave it to his Queen, Eleanor, in 1280 but the 'Camel' derivation is less certain. Enter it from north or south through a double right-angle, to ½ mile (0.8km) street of creamy-grey houses, mainly in short groups of three or four, with each house different from its neighbours in the row. Sizes, heights and gables also differ, so there is always a lively variety. Wooden lintels, some white, some black, span windows, small upstairs, larger below. Pantile, small clay tile or thatch cover roofs, and chimney-stacks are brick. West of the church, Church Path is a cobbled causeway of grey stone. Grace Martin's Lane on the east is the most ostentatiously attractive group in this very pleasing village where front gardens are the rule rather than the exception. West Camel, a mile (1.6km) away, is smaller, more rural, but with nice houses near the church.

Eastwards are the hilly lands of Arthurian legend. Cadbury Castle looks down on the warm stone cottages of South Cadbury, closely clustered near the church. Cadbury Chapel, by the main road, now a private house, confirms in its banded wall the close link between the Lias and the oolite. Castle Farm, opposite a stony track once called Arthur's Lane, has stone mullions and lintels, a 1687 datestone, and an extension built with smaller, poorer quality stones, and wooden lintels. Brick has been insensitively used in recent development, but at nearby Compton Pauncefoot, more care has been shown; the tawny stone has been used in the 1825 Gothic castle and the contemporary, whimsically urban, tiny crescent of five cottages. Within a few miles, Charlton

Queen Camel, Somerset. Grey stone of the Blue Lias in a long street village

Horethorne, the Cheritons, and Bratton Seymour, greenly wrapped in orchards and lush pastures, pick out the theme of greyer limestone, emphasising how, according to their geographical position, villages along the writhing Lias are faithful to their own stone.

Not until north Oxfordshire does the brown Lias reassert itself, consolidating its effect on landscape and buildings across the Northamptonshire uplands. The A361 from Chipping Norton to Banbury is an excellent approach from the south-west, with growing Banbury itself a good centre for marlstone meanderings. East of Chipping Norton are Enstone, the Tews, the Bartons, and Sandford St Martin. Now that it is a conservation area it is hoped that Great Tew will recover from the dereliction afflicting it a few years ago. Village, church, 'big house', farms and parkland form a rare example of wholesale landscape improvement, planned by J. C. Loudon in 1808. Opposing the common practice then of removing villages out of sight of the new big house and its park, he thought that existing cottages, with gardens back and front, contributed to the amenities. Some of Great Tew's cottages are seventeenth-century, and Loudon left them. Others were given rustic porches in the 1820s, and today, mellow, iron-tinted stone houses, some thatched, some stone-slated, harmonise with neat greens and mature trees. The eighteenth-century Falkland Arms looks across to a gabled Victorian school with adjoining teacher's house. Although many cottages were built in the nineteenth century, they continue the older traditional style, with drip-moulds over the windows, moulded door-frames, and neat little gabled dormers here and there.

Victorian, too, are the houses at Sandford St Martin, rebuilding in a characteristic 'closed' village, again completely traditional in style. Hook Norton, to the north, has spread along its valley, leaving church and main street on the hillside. At Scotland End, on the western edge of the village, Hook Norton's proudly independent brewery occupies a handsome range of ironstone buildings in which it produces its own excellent beer. To the north, Sibford Ferris has a quietly dignified main street with farmsteads on one side and Home Close (1911) on the other: Sibford Gower's manor-house, now called Old Court House, has thatched dormers, while Shutford retains memories of its plush industry which thrived there for two hundred years. Early this century it was the only source in the world for Wrench's hand-woven livery plush which graced royal houses and courts of Europe. Nearby, Epwell is a quiet little place of steep-pitched brown stone houses clustered round a spring in a steep-sided valley.

Wroxton lies just off the A422 Banbury–Stratford road, its main street lined with steep grassy banks topped with thatched cottages of rust-coloured Hornton stone. Wooden lintels are commoner than stone ones, but the ethos of stone continues at ground level in a cobbled causeway leading to the churchyard gate. Opposite, the former church barn is now a house, and throughout the village honeysuckle and roses decorate front gardens and walls. West of the village a 1686 signpost has fingers pointing to the three nearest market towns and London. Northwards from the main road lanes lead to Hornton, several feet above the neighbouring fields. Thirty years ago they were on the same level, but beds of ironstone beneath the surface have been worked and quarried, the removed topsoil replaced, and the land lowered as much as 20ft (6m).

Hornton itself lies at the valley head of one of the Sor Brook feeder streams, sheltered from the north by a hanging beech wood. Mature trees almost obscure houses dispersed around its green; mild echoes of Cotswold vernacular are revealed in stone mullions and lintels, with wooden lintels used on more modest houses. Thatch, stone-slate and tile add variety to roofs, and behind the church cottages and their colourful gardens occupy old quarries. Many villages in the stone belt which gave their name to a superb building stone won from local quarries are in themselves slightly disappointing. Not so Hornton, for in situation, layout, colour and style, it is quietly memorable. So is Horley, 2 miles (3.2km) down the valley, on a spur, with steep-gabled cottages bordering a lane winding up a hill, and a number of thoughtfully designed modern terraces.

Hornton, Oxfordshire. Warm brown stone with stone mullions and drip-moulds; deep thatch, gay gardens and stone walls

South of Banbury, Bloxham's splendid-steepled church beckons travellers along the busy A361, a former agricultural village which turned to plush-weaving last century and commuterdom today. Brown stone houses line both sides of the road with narrow lanes of close-set cottages leading from it. A thatched court-house in the churchyard testifies to Bloxham's former borough status. On the A423, 3 miles (4.8km) distant, Deddington, too, was a market town, but, unlike Bloxham, retains its large market square, empty except for vehicles, and an early nineteenth-century town hall. Seventeenth- and eighteenth-century inns, houses and humble cottages face the square, or are tucked away behind stone walls. New Street now carries the main road, but Church Street and Castle Street are worth walking.

Adderbury, two minutes' drive to the north, is divided by the Sor Brook into two – East Adderbury, which is flanked by the same A423 which afflicts Deddington, and suffers accordingly, and West Adderbury, much the quieter. Each has a manor-house, each a green, and each some attractive, thatched ironstone cottages, interspersed with larger seventeenth-century and Georgian houses indicative of rising prosperity through agriculture, and, later, the clothing trade.

Across the Cherwell the best of Aynho lies just off the A41, where traffic grinds up the hill past an attractive group of cottages. From The Square, Little Lane and Holloway are enticements to explore the quiet parts of this beautiful, cared-for village. Dove-grey and golden limestone reveal contrasting tones and textures; cottages show informal variety, and apricot trees are trained up sunlit walls. Almshouses, a former seventeenth-century grammar school, Aynho House and park, and the early eighteenth-century church add particular distinction to one of Northamptonshire's finest villages.

North of Banbury a salient of marlstone thrusts northwards into the lowland Lias clays of the Feldon, but Warwickshire claims from its Oxfordshire neighbour three villages on this eastward spur of the Edge Hills, and one below the western scarp. All are of ochre-coloured ironstone – Radway's stone terraces beneath a green look upwards to Sanderson Miller's octagonal, embattled Edge Hill Tower, built 1746–50 as a place where he could entertain his friends on the spot where Charles I's standard stood in October 1642 prior to the battle which took place on the fields below. East of the folly tower and its enfolding beechwoods, Ratley's ironstone houses step gently down to a tiny green.

Edge Hill's ridge road swings eastwards, as Camp Lane, to the A41 near Warmington, which now bypasses this most beautiful of Warwickshire's marlstone villages, snugly sheltered beneath its hilltop church. Houses of Hornton stone loosely surround a spacious triangular manicured green, with the large town pool (formerly used for sheep-dipping) almost too formal in perfection. South of the pond the huge, gabled, late Tudor manor-house presents its shadowed northern façade to the village, a dominating silhouette

Aynho

for most of the year, but on early summer days a glowing study of textured stone in mullions and massive chimney-breast, picked out by the morning sun. House roofs of stone and slate and thatch, white-painted woodwork, and a shade too careful restoration emphasise Warmington's picture-postcard appeal. Nearby, Shotteswell – 'Satchel', locally – is a friendly jumble of brown stone cottages, with a church on a steep slope.

The A361 is a useful road for following the Lias north-eastwards from Banbury to Daventry, moving into Northamptonshire on the way. The road insinuates itself through Wardington, last of the Oxfordshire villages, winding past Wardington Manor's high walls and gables, and the steep-pitched, thatched roofs of gabled cottages. Beyond the church, the village widens to a green, almost a welcome relief after the enclosing stone.

Some brick has intruded at Chipping Warden without seriously disqualifying it as a good, attractive stone village. A convex curve of cottages follows the main road opposite a high-stepped plinth supporting merely the base of a medieval cross. Short, neat rows of brown stone cottages near the church are thatched, slated, or tiled, and Mill Lane invites exploration. Other lanes leading north-west from the A361 are equally tempting, although the villages they serve, the Boddingtons, Priors Hardwick and Priors Marston, have only a few stone cottages amid a predominance of brick. Here, the Oxford Canal follows a contour course round Wormleighton Hill, where the estate housing

of Wormleighton village adjoins the impressive gatehouse of the manor-house. Some seventeenth-century houses survive, brown stone, with drip-moulds; clusters of chimney-stacks — lines of four, or squares of four — dominate rooftops.

Back on the main road, Byfield is an extensive nucleated village with some stone houses and more recent brick ones. Charwelton, 2 miles (3.2km) onwards, retains a late medieval packhorse bridge 3ft (1m) wide, spanning the Cherwell, and made redundant when the main road was slightly realigned. Badby, from a distance, appears to be brick-built, but a short detour from the A361 shows a number of attractive ironstone houses, many thatched, widely dispersed round a broad green, focused on the former school and school-house with its low tower, yet given some cohesion by virtue of the cottages built in groups. Some have stone-mullioned windows and neat drip-moulds above windows, but occasional thatch is often rather tatty.

East of the A361 is the undulating landscape of the Northamptonshire Wolds, whose light soils, favourable for cultivation, have resulted in an even settlement pattern, with villages spaced rarely more than 2 or 3 miles (3.2 or 4.8km) apart, linked by winding lanes between small fields. Preston Capes and Farthingstone have pleasant groups of ironstone cottages in characteristic Northamptonshire style, without ostentation, and frequently without front gardens. But the greyer oolite is never far away, and at Blisworth, some miles farther east, both stones are used in a number of houses in alternate bands, often with quite large, squarish blocks in each. The polychrome effect is pleasing when seen in only occasional buildings, but too 'busy' and disturbing in the mass. Steep-pitched roofs of thatch predominate, and one house on the Stoke Bruerne road is distinguished by its three-light mullioned windows, now blocked in on the ground and first floors of its gable end. As with other ironstone houses, lintels are of wood, chimney-stacks of brick, although the seventeenth-century 'Stoneacres' uses the grey oolite for its dressings.

Ashby St Ledgers, north of Daventry, is in Catesby country, and local legend asserts that in an upper room of the timbered gatehouse to the medieval manor behind the church the Gunpowder Plot was hatched in 1605, by Robert Catesby and his conspirators. The village itself, a few hundred yards from the M1, looks older than it is. The Coach and Horses Inn, formerly a sixteenth-century farmhouse, was Victorianised late last century, contemporary with the estate cottages which comprise most of the village. Ironstone-rubble walls, some capped with tiles, steep-pitched roofs of thatch, and

---

(opposite)

Warmington, Warwickshire. Brown stone, manicured lawns, and well-behaved ducks in a tidy pond: the picture is too pristine, perhaps

Chipping Warden, Northamptonshire. Rubble brown stone, roughly coursed. Wooden lintels and a bread oven by the door

Blisworth, Northamptonshire. Banded ironstone and limestone used decoratively

beautifully kept front gardens and greens ensure approbation of visitors prepared to accept it all as a slice of 'olde England'.

North of Northampton, the Lias belt takes a slightly more northerly course and East Haddon continues the theme of ironstone and thatch – even the village pump is thatched. Harlestone, on the Althorp estates, still has its own working quarry in the Althorp grounds, with village housing, particularly along the main road, showing squirearchal influence, although pebble-dash and superficial decoration seem to be an unnecessary treatment of good stonework. Pitsford, within a few hundred yards of a large reservoir, and too near to Northampton for comfort, has managed to keep its village integrity, its ironstone houses showing a good variety of roof lines. The grey limestone frontage of The Griffin Inn anticipates the two-tone buildings a few miles to the north, beyond Rockingham Forest.

Sheet 141 of the Ordnance Survey 1:50,000 Series underlines the truth of Sir Thomas Fuller's claim three centuries ago that 'especially seeing England presents thee with so many observables'. Near its centre, Corby grew on the Northamptonshire ironstone, really a ferruginous sandstone heavily exploited by open-cast mining. Iron-stained limestones of the Lias have been used extensively in villages west of Kettering and Corby, and to the north of the River Welland, but with the grey or cream oolite never being very far away, especially with the navigable river for transport of small loads, it is this oolite which has been used for dressings and mouldings round doors and windows and chimneys, with the rust-coloured ironstone, occasionally ashlared, more usually rubble, for walls. Alternate bands of dark and light stone feature prominently not only in houses but in some churches, and, most strikingly, in that quirkiest of English oddities, Sir Thomas Tresham's Triangular Lodge a mile (1.6km) west of Rushton village between Kettering and Desborough.

Gretton stands on the edge of the Northamptonshire uplands, apparently high above the Welland valley – although there is scarcely a couple of hundred feet difference in height. Narrow streets packed with small cottages of ironstone surround a village green which retains its stocks and whipping-post. A few miles south-west, Cottingham's cottages seem to be pale in tone, liberally endowed with inns and hotels, and with wide Welland-scape views. Between these villages is Rockingham, neither of the uplands nor of the vale, but linking the two, its long single street descending the hill in a shallow curve between grassy borders and tawny cottages with thatch or Collyweston slates. Though dignified, spacious and colourful, Rockingham has two faults – a busy main road, which makes it unquiet, and a too open nature, leaving no secret corners to discover. Its castle looks down on the village and below it is the church, with no architectural merit and no apparent relationship with the village, so an exploration of Rockingham amounts to a walk up one side of the road and down the other, which reveals datestones from 1663 to 1795. Stone mullions and dressings are the exception; white-painted wooden lintels, white woodwork of doors and windows and gay flower-borders certainly enhance by contrast the warm-toned stone.

Across the Welland is Leicestershire, although in this part old Rutland loyalties remain strong. The A6003 continues northwards to Uppingham and Oakham, and to its west, and roughly as far north as the A47 Leicester–Uppingham road, many villages contain a good proportion of ironstone houses, increasingly interspersed with brick. Scarcely any such dilution mars the subtly curving long main street of Lyddington, just off the A6003, undoubtedly one of the best of the Midlands marlstone villages. For over ½ mile (0.8km) both sides of the street glow with warm stone buildings of the seventeenth and eighteenth centuries, and, unlike those at Rockingham, butting on to the pavement. The Bay House, south of the church, is outstanding, with grey limestone for all dressings and the bay itself, carrying a datestone of 1656, with a thatched roof completing the harmony. Lyndon House is most unusual in having ironstone mullions; later, smaller cottages revert to wooden lintels. The street widens to a broad green north of the church, with the stump of a medieval cross-shaft, but Lyddington's former importance was related to the bishops of Lincoln from about 1200, having a manor-house there, rebuilt during the last decades of the fifteenth century, at the same time as Bishop Russell rebuilt the nave of the church. The manor was converted into a hospital in 1602, since when it has been known as the Bede House which adjoins the north side of the churchyard, warm-stoned, with grey oolite liberally used in buttresses, dressings and chimneys, all darkened during sunny days as the shadow of the church tower moves caressingly along its front. A neat little polygonal watch-tower at the angle of the manorial precinct projects on to the pavement at a corner of the main street, marlstone, grey-stone quoined, with a pyramidal slate roof, and an archway for pedestrians.

West of the main road, Great Easton's High Street, more compact than Lyddington's, has many good houses of iron-tinted marlstone, mainly with oolite dressings, but Medbourne, whose attractions are enhanced by trees and a stream spanned by a remarkably elegant medieval footbridge near the church, has brick intrusions into its stony nucleus. To the north, Hallaton is the largest village in this ironstone quadrant of the county, at the focus of five local roads which helped to support its former market status.

No main trunk roads are near enough to intrude seriously upon Hallaton's relative remoteness, so that its identity survives, and it is a 'villagey' village, with an attractive High Street, shops used by local folk, and sufficient old buildings to allow it to indulge in memories. Streets converge on 'The Cross', a small triangular green with a strange, conical stone butter cross, and surrounded by neat stone houses, some thatched. The older houses along the road to the church are also ironstone, some stone-mullioned and dressed with oolite, and Georgian ones of brick.

Across the A47 to the north, and beyond the Eye Brook, Belton's streets form a square, with the church near its centre on a diagonal. Ironstone cottages

*(opposite)*_____

Lyddington, Leicestershire. A superb linear village with many two-tone houses with stone dressings and brown stone walls, as in the gazebo of the Bede House with its pedestrian archway and *(below)* seventeenth-century Bede House, summer home of the bishops of Lincoln, shows the light and dark stone arrangement which is so visually attractive

predominate, the best near the church, round the war memorial, and in Nether Street. Some grey oolite, and some bits of brick have been used to repair walls, steep-pitched roofs of Collyweston slates were probably once thatched, and a maypole is still prominent at the centre of this workaday village once famed for its fair where great shire-horses were bought and sold. Although much of eastern Leicestershire is on the marlstone, it is largely overlain with deposits of clays and sands, resulting in brick buildings predominating, and as one travels northwards Collyweston slates give way to pantiles, used to roof cottages of brick or creamy-grey limestone, and the golden Lias of the Midlands is gradually left behind.

While the influence of the Lias diminishes north of Leicestershire, about 20 miles (32km) to the west another, older, limestone starts to make its presence felt. On the Geological Survey Ten Mile Map a narrow band of bright blue runs northwards from Nottingham to the mouth of the Tyne, representing the extent of the English dolomite, a limestone laid down in Permian seas about two hundred million years ago, in which some of its constituent calcium carbonate was replaced by magnesium carbonate, giving this stone both its name, magnesian limestone, and its distinctive creamy-whiteness. Very fine grained and, like other limestones, soft when quarried but hardening on exposure to the air, its ability to take crisp, detailed cutting made it popular with medieval masons. Unfortunately, it is badly affected by chemical pollution, and since its course is so frequently bordered by that of the coalfields of northern England and their associated developments of the past two centuries, resulting in such pollution, magnesian limestone has not been greatly used for vernacular buildings.

Thus, although the narrow dolomite ridge runs for almost 150 miles (241km), producing a landscape of gently rolling hills rarely reaching 500ft (152m) in height, with well-drained soils, rich farmlands and generously wooded parks, only rarely are its villages built almost entirely of this stone. Paradoxically, it has provided north-eastern England with a fine inheritance of cathedrals, churches, castles and halls well meriting its description – in a purely Yorkshire context – as 'the aristocrat among them all' (building stones). York Minster, the walls and gateways of York, Bolsover Castle, Worksop Priory, Roche Abbey, the two great medieval churches at Beverley, Conisbrough Castle, are all built of the proud white limestone.

Northbound travellers on the M1 north of Nottingham see the dolomite ridge mainly to their east. The M18 slices through it near Rotherham, and the A1 follows it very closely through South and North Yorkshire, and across the Tees into Durham, where the limestone broadens out north-eastwards to form the coastline between Hartlepool and South Shields. A more leisurely journey through small towns and villages reveals the extent to which the limestone has been used locally. Worksop is a good starting point, and between it and the M1 a number of villages contain groups or terraces of cottages, invariably of

Plate 3 Ashby St Ledgers, Northamptonshire. Nineteenth-century estate housing, ironstone rubble, steeply-pitched thatched roofs, broad green verges

Plate 4 Malham, North Yorkshire. Rubble limestone walls, white-painted sandstone dressings, low-pitched roofs of sandstone flags. All in a largely mid-Victorian estate village

modest proportions, of warm yellow, sometimes pink-tinged, stones with wooden lintels and pantiled roofs. Nether Langwith, near Bolsover, with a stream down its street, Whitwell to its north, which has managed to remain reasonably unspoilt, and Barlborough within a shout of the motorway, have their eighteenth-century hearts gradually becoming swamped with new brick-built estates. The Anstons to the north have lost the battle, but the much more rural Letwell is characteristic of the magnesian limestone landscape, a small village whose size has scarcely changed through two centuries, and retaining a high proportion of largely eighteenth-century houses and cottages of local stone.

Indeed, one of South Yorkshire's pleasant surprises is the remarkably rural countryside still existing so close to the coalfield and industrial developments between Doncaster, Rotherham, Barnsley and Wakefield. Fertile soils of the limestone were attractive to early settlers, so villages were relatively thick on the ground. Parishes have remained small, and among these High Melton, Hickleton, Marr, Brodsworth, Burgwallis and Thorpe Salvin have all retained village identity. But Hooton Pagnell is the best, a farming village at the heart of its parish, its main north-south street broadening to a triangular village green, with the proud limestone church and adjacent hall prominent on the escarpment, above a grassy bank golden with April daffodils. The village butter cross and pound by the green contribute to the scene, and almost all the village houses are of stone, stepped down the hillside, pantiled, with timber lintels and some like Home Farm, have chamfered stone mullions and drip-moulds typical of the early Stuart period.

To the north-east, across the A1, Campsall is an expanding village whose church has one of Yorkshire's finest Norman towers. Over the road is the stone-built vicarage, adapted from a fifteenth-century manor-house, while Arksey, Kirk Smeaton, Womersley and Darrington continue the theme of handsome churches dominating villages where local limestone is used only in a few older farms and barns. Not until the Wharfe is reached near Wetherby do the villages show a more general use of dolomite. Bramham, Clifford, Boston Spa and Thorp Arch have groups, terraces and individual houses, almost all of eighteenth- and nineteenth-century date. Bramham is a village for sauntering. A dolomite-pebble throw from the A1, and leading from its central square, narrow lanes and streets are bordered by cottages of creamy limestone, pantiled, with small windows, and restricted views. Low Way leads to the church; other short streets drop steeply down to it, and even the speeding motorist on the A1 has time to glimpse the vividness of Bramham's clean stone gleaming in afternoon sunlight.

A mile (1.6km) away, Clifford has rows of artisans' stone cottages, while at Boston Spa Georgian houses adorn the High Street, their columnar porches and bow-windows reminders of two centuries ago when visitors came to take the waters of this modest little town above the River Wharfe. On the opposite

Hooton Pagnell, South Yorkshire. Pale magnesian limestone, rubble-walled, beneath pink pantiled or stone-slate roofs. Large sandstone lintels. Roof rhythm of a village on a hillside and *(opposite)* Well, North Yorkshire. Mid-eighteenth-century Latimer Almshouses in a delightful, stream-blessed village

bank, Thorp Arch's single street has a small green at the lower end, and paired mid-nineteenth-century houses of local stone, slate-roofed, with distinctive gable windows, round-headed or in Venetian style, and tall brick chimneys clustered usually in groups of six. To the east, Newton Kyme is a tiny village at the entrance to a fine park, with a handful of stately Georgian houses west of Newton Hall, illustrating the ashlared quality of magnesian limestone. Down-river, Tadcaster's Roman name, Calcaria, is significant, and the great dolomite quarries which mar nearby rural landscapes are worked mainly for agricultural lime, and no longer is the Wharfe used as a water highway for the transport of this noble building stone to more distant parts of Yorkshire beyond. Within the triangle between Wetherby, Selby and Pontefract, almost every village church is of this local stone, so that a journey in the area becomes a pilgrimage from one proud white tower to the next, those at Sherburn-in-

Elmet and Bolton Percy being particularly noteworthy, while Healaugh's south doorway shows sumptuous Norman carving. Brayton's slender tower, crowned with a neat octagon and delicate spire, points the way to Selby, but this, and the other villages, have stone used in only a minority of houses.

The narrow belt of dolomite continues its wriggling course northwards beyond Knaresborough, keeping a few miles west of the A1 until Catterick Bridge. Rich farmlands in a gently undulating landscape form the quiet setting for unostentatiously attractive villages of which West Tanfield is particularly worthwhile. Seen from the bridge across the Ure its group of fifteenth-century church and Marmion gatehouse tower, pink-pantiled stone cottages with gardens sloping down to the riverside meadows and trees, is undeniably memorable. A few miles to the north Well and Snape also have pleasant groups of eighteenth- and nineteenth-century cottages, where, as at West Tanfield, the limestone has a yellowish-buff tinge to it.

Beyond the Tees, the dolomite fans out north-eastwards, and produces, at Marsden Rock near South Shields, its most dramatic outcrop — cliffs and sea-stacks, arched, creviced and pockmarked, the home of thousands of seabirds. But as a building material to provide homes in south-east Durham, the same stone has rarely been used since early last century. Occasional farms and barns, and the odd eighteenth-century cottage, remind us of what once was, but industrial developments during Victorian times on and near the coalfield coincided with the almost exclusive use of brick. In a county where any sort of rural village can come as a surprise, Heighington is worth singling out. Situated almost 500ft (152m) up on the magnesian limestone ridge, it is a classic example of the Durham green-village, although its layout is more apparent in the plan, or in an aerial view, than on the ground, since the Norman church and churchyard are near the middle of the north side of the large rectangular green, dividing it into two unequal parts. Other small groups of buildings have intruded south of the churchyard, but nevertheless the green gives a visual unity, and roads entering it at opposite corners, and in the middle of two sides, are so placed that views from the stone, colour-washed, or brick houses are inwards. None sees the fields beyond, although the back lane right round the houses is a survival of the medieval access from village houses to the common fields.

4
Mountain Limestone

With the limestone areas already described, the deep harmony between villages and the landscape is one in which buildings play the major role. Their setting, though important, never intrudes. Moving into the older limestones, called by geologists the Carboniferous Limestones, but more conveniently thought of as Mountain Limestones since they are associated with upland areas of the north and west, the reverse applies. Although there is still a satisfying harmony, it is the landscape which takes the leading part. We go to the Cotswolds for the charm and quiet tranquillity of their villages and gracious buildings, but to the White Peak of Derbyshire, to the Yorkshire Dales, and to the Mendips of Somerset for their natural limestone wonders, the scars, crags and tors, caves, pot-holes and waterfalls, and the wide windy uplands intersected by green valleys with clean, sparkling rivers.

Villages tend to be incidental, though usually attractive. The Mountain Limestones are often associated with mineral deposits, especially lead-ore, which in all three areas mentioned has been exploited over many centuries. Limestone itself is useful to man, as building material and as the source of lime for mortar, cement and fertiliser. As a result, many villages in the limestone country have seen their share of industry, and the scars of old workings are rarely far away.

Mountain Limestone is much harder than oolite, and although its use as a building stone is widespread, it was never thought good enough to be worth carrying beyond its areas of origin. Its hardness made detailed carving very difficult so that buildings made of it lack any urbanity or ornamentation, and it was rarely used for important buildings. Few village churches are built of it. Its hardness also meant that it was not very suitable for making good, square-cut corner-stones, so that frequently, particularly where a sandstone or gritstone was reasonably handy, those would be used for quoins, door-jambs and lintels, and window-dressings. In Derbyshire and Yorkshire houses of Mountain Limestone almost invariably have roofs of sandstone flags, the materials together creating buildings and villages sturdy, forceful and roughly textured, completely in keeping with the landscape, with the landscape having the last word.

Few villages break the austere skyline of the Mendip plateau in north Somerset. Priddy is loosely dispersed round its large, irregular green, while near the western end of the hills pockmarked landscapes around Shipham, another green-village, and Rowberrow are reminders of the vanished zinc industry which prospered early last century. Former miners' cottages are now snapped up by Bristol commuters. Blagdon and Burrington look northwards from the lower slopes of Mendip, their close-clustered cottage groups mainly white or colour-washed to brighten the otherwise cool grey stone. Pantile roofs predominate and add to the colour, while at Compton Martin and the Harptree villages, rendering and colour-wash continue to disguise the local stone, although at West Harptree the church and two impressive seventeenth-century houses are of pinkish sandstone.

Chewton Mendip by the main Bath–Wells road is dominated by the splendour of its soaring church tower, throwing into sharper contrast the small stone cottages of the village in its hollow near the source of the River Chew. Its gentler setting gives it a softer appearance than other lead-mining villages, as does that of Litton, a mile (1.6km) to the north.

Gurney Slade is a quarry village, but to the north-eastern part of Mendip, where deep valleys dissect the uplands, coal was mined from the early nineteenth century until 1973. The legacy of hundreds of small early pits and almost eighty deep mines is revealed less in the landscape than in the buildings. Villages and hamlets proliferated, so that today little rows of stone cottages form part of most rural settlements. Though none is outstanding, they present a picture of one side of Mendip's more recent past to merit a visit which could conveniently include Holcombe, Coleford and Vobster in the south, to Farrington Gurney, Hallatrow, High Littleton and Farmborough in the north. Throughout, austerity prevails. Terraces are more common than groups, and stone of different sizes is used in house walls. Brick is occasionally preferred for door- and window-openings, and some houses have small, flat-topped dormers. Pantiles add their own colour and texture to help make these villages of north Somerset and Avon visually more attractive than those in most coal-mining localities.

While Mendip villages over the past two centuries have largely depended on a single industry for their livelihood, those of Derbyshire's limestone uplands often reflect the former dual economy of farming and lead-mining. South of the Hope Valley on the edge of the Peak District National Park is the area known as Low Peak, or White Peak because of its many outcrops of pale grey limestone. A thin layer of soil covers the domed grassy plateau which rises to around 1,400ft (427m) and rarely drops below 900ft (274m). Drystone walls, brilliant white in sunlight, chequer the wind-swept hills, farms and settlements seek shelter of shallow folds, shelter-belts occasionally break smooth skylines, and the austerity of the landscape is relieved by deep, narrow, sinuous valleys, the beautiful Derbyshire Dales.

Ashbourne, Matlock and Buxton are at the corners of a triangle which embraces much of the limestone country of southern Derbyshire, in which

Tissington, a few miles north of Ashbourne, is an admirable aperitif. Usually approached from the A515 between large gatepiers and along an avenue of lime trees in a parkland setting, it is clearly an estate village with early nineteenth-century houses harmonising with their older neighbours, all cottagey behind broad grassed areas. A noble stand of beeches and sycamores overlooks a triangular duck pond near the former school of 1837. Coursed limestone with sandstone quoins and dressings for the houses, together with limestone walls, and five eighteenth-century wells decoratively dressed on Ascension Day with mosses and flowers, create a controlled composition watched over by a handsome Norman church and the Jacobean Tissington Hall, home of the Fitzherberts since 1611.

To the north-east, Parwich is nicely set in the hills, a limestone village with plenty of excellent eighteenth-century houses, two- and three-storey, with sandstone quoins and dressings, many having neat drip-moulds above windows, on copings, and as kneelers. Greens add softness to the setting but Parwich Hall, 1747, slightly above the village centre, is an unusually intrusive, though elegant, brick structure. Eastwards is Brassington at the centre of a complex web of lanes and tracks, a fascinating example of an organic community which adapted and grew to meet changing economic circumstances. The church tower of 1200, as well as the Tudor House and Gate Inn in Tower Street, early Jacobean, are of a fawn-coloured limestone, but the rest of the houses – miners' and quarrymen's cottages, farms and nonconformist chapels – are of pale grey limestone, with little or no ostentation. Approaching Carsington from the south gives the most rewarding view of this village at the

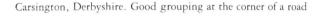

Carsington, Derbyshire. Good grouping at the corner of a road

wooded foot of a south-facing hill. Three rows of two- and three-storey houses, the front ones with good gardens, are individually unspectacular, but informally grouped present an attractive scene.

Bonsall, near Matlock, is vastly different. It is situated at the head of a short dry valley which has dictated the elongated shape of the village, with a widening at the centre an obvious nucleus. Here, the village cross on its thirteen-stepped plinth is dated 1671, a time when Bonsall was experiencing some prosperity, also evidenced by a number of buildings in the area around the cross of about the same date. A beam in the bar of the King's Head – gabled with finials, and stone-mullioned windows – is dated 1677, and although a number of nearby buildings have been refronted, a view of their sides and backs reveals windows similar to those of the inn. Lead-mining in the area flourished during the late seventeenth century and throughout most of the eighteenth century, carried out by farmer-miners. When the water-powered cotton-spinning mills developed at nearby Cromford in the 1770s, many local inhabitants started to work there, although domestic framework knitting was already a village industry in Bonsall. There is a good surviving example of a small stone-built workshop, dated 1737, with a long window in an upper storey reached by an outside stone stairway. Puddle Hill, in Bonsall Dale, was probably a complete little mining settlement, and the school nearby was endowed in 1718, with master's house adjoining, all remodelled last century. Bonsall's houses and workshops are humble, appropriate to a self-grown

Bonsall, Derbyshire. Seventeenth-century houses in the market place. Limestone rubble-walling, sandstone quoins, dressings and finials, and a sandstone stepped cross

industrial village. Rendering gives protection to poor quality limestone, although sandstone dressings were commonly used for door- and window-openings, and in the many field barns on the moor beyond the village. Perhaps to save space and to give a southern aspect, a number of Bonsall's houses have their gable-ends to the road, and, even in a cramped valley setting, many have small gardens.

Winster, though prospering later than Bonsall, has an entirely different character, and is the best surviving eighteenth-century mining settlement in the Peak District. Although its population of just over 1,000 in 1841 was 300 less than Bonsall's, its compact form, concentrated along a single main street, contained many three-storey houses, creating an impressive urban appearance which still prevails. Such properties were the farmhouses and residences of prosperous mine owners and ore-traders, the smaller ones on the Banks being those of the copers (who took bargains to work other people's mines), or smaller miners. Among the best buildings are the seventeenth-century Dower House at the west end of Main Street, Winster Hall on the north side of the street, Palladian and pretentious, with the essential quality of masonry adornment characteristic of much larger houses. At the east end of the street a pair of houses disguised as a single property show similar characteristics. Half-way along the street, and an obvious focal point, is the market hall, pointed sixteenth-century arcades below, a brick upper storey with, unusually, stone mullioned and transomed windows. This was the National Trust's first Derbyshire property.

Limestone villages in the White Peak tend to be linear, their shape dictated by the nature of the landscape or the water supply, often along a spring line where the limestone meets the shale. Elton, on the moor's edge west of Winster, is no exception, but is unusual in being on a strata boundary, with houses on the north side of the street on gritstone, those opposite on limestone. House walls, and even more apparently, the gardens, reflect the dichotomy, with azaleas on the gritstone and lime-loving flowers on the limestone. Among many rugged cottages are some which were prosperous farmhouses, built during the first half of the eighteenth century in a style already seen at Winster, with mullioned windows, a projecting string course, and a decorated doorway. Greengates Farm of 1747, now two houses, is a good example, with well-faced limestone walls, gritstone quoins and dressings, and neat chimneys. The Old Hall opposite, now a youth hostel, is of two dates, 1668 and 1715, and, like other buildings on the south side, has its front facing south and turns its back to the street.

About 3 miles (4.8km) north, Bradford Dale has a trio of good limestone villages, Youlgreave being the largest and most important, extending along a shelf above the River Bradford, with one of the best of Peakland churches whose situation creates a slight dog-leg in the long main street. Although there is a good group of eighteenth-century houses nearby, the best buildings

Middleton-by-Youlgreave, Derbyshire. Eighteenth-century buildings form a satisfying group on the edge of the village

are to the west, Old Hall of 1656, a small manor-house with hall and cross-wings, and Old Hall Farm behind it, 1630, of hall and single cross-wing. The huge, tub-shaped Conduit Head, 1829, centrally placed and fed from springs behind the village, still provides Youlgreave with its water supply.

To the east, where the Bradford meets the villageless Lathkill Dale, Alport nestles in a wooded valley just off the road. Stonecrop graces limestone walls, there is honeysuckle and cultivated gardens, a very narrow packhorse bridge over a sparkling river, and groups of charming cottages. The seventeenth-century Monk's Hall has a fine gabled front, and, were it not for sandstone dressings imparting two-tone harmony, this could easily be a corner of Cotswold country.

Middleton-by-Youlgreave is largely an early nineteenth-century estate village with tall sycamores and neat groups of cottages set about a triangular open space which ought to have been a green. Beyond an excellent modern conversion near the tiny, little-used chapel of St Michael, is a particularly good range of farm buildings, and a nearby track leads down to the infant river whose 2 mile (3.2km) course ensures that it never reaches maturity. The ruins of Middleton's old pumping station, now roofless, show even in decay the fine quality of traditional building materials using local limestone.

The Ordnance Survey 1:25,000 Leisure Map 'The White Peak' covers two sides of paper measuring almost 4 × 3ft (1.2 × 1m), a superb piece of draughtsmanship and detail. In the area around Monyash, Flagg, Taddington and Chelmorton it shows a wonderful pattern of short straight lines indicating the limestone walls enclosing the former open fields of these parishes. Mostly of late eighteenth-century construction, they represented the final acts of an enclosure process which had been under way for centuries. A journey through this landscape is a pertinent reminder of the enormous amounts of stone used and the laborious process of actual building. Without the walls the bleakness of these grassy uplands would be greatly intensified. They add, even at two centuries remove, the essential element of human endeavour.

Monyash is one of the best examples in these limestone landscapes of a nucleated village. Sitting in a shallow fold, its houses cluster round a cross-roads, with church, school, inn, and a spacious green and a pond, all reflecting a past importance. It was granted a charter in 1340 for a market and fair, and for centuries was an important lead-mining centre, but a busy past has given way to a quiet present. Monyash has a distinctive character, with good examples of small-scale domestic architecture. Houses are of limestone, with all the detail and decoration on gritstone dressings. Some drip-mouldings are, unusually, a couple of feet above windows; copings crown gables; there are robust chimneys and occasional string courses. A surprising number of mullioned windows have survived well into the eighteenth century, and the Bull's Head Inn is probably the oldest building apart from the church.

To the north-west Chelmorton is linear, in a landscape of lines, appreciated best from the brow of the hill to the south or from the lane above the eastern side of the village. Surprisingly, Chelmorton lies between 1,100ft (335m) and 1,250ft (381m), with the church at its highest, northern end, and pearl-grey stone farmhouses, windowless barns and austere cottages strung out along both sides of a single, slightly curving street. Some houses, especially near the church, have their gables to the street, but few show any eighteenth-century architectural pretensions. However, some recent council houses do continue the traditional style of building. Behind the farms and houses, particularly on the east side, are elongated narrow crofts each one generally as wide as the street frontage of a single farmstead. Sometimes, adjacent fields have been amalgamated to double their width, but the overall pattern prevails. Unfortunately, records do not exist which can definitely prove whether the field pattern is a survival from medieval days, whether it represents a late Tudor expansion, or whether it is the outcome of enclosures of the parish commons in 1805. But, like primroses on a river bank, its appeal is strongly visual without the need to be academic.

Taddington, across the hill to the north, lies along a shelf, with wide views northwards beyond the wooded gorge of the Wye to the distant shadowed moorlands of the Dark Peak. Its long, unplanned street has houses, cottages, farms and barns sharing a basic similarity but with individual treatment.

Limestone is the common denominator, but gritstone dressings allow variety. Generally, the scale is modest but dwarfed by a big fourteenth-century church splendidly aloof on the north side of the village, its tower in gritstone, the rest limestone with gritstone dressings characteristic of the nearness of two different geological strata. Few areas in England show the two-tone contrasts in local stone so well as this White Peak area of Derbyshire.

A few miles down the valley of the Wye, Ashford-in-the-Water is one of the few Peakland villages which merit being called charming. The river has given it a reason for existence and is a convenient barrier separating it from the A6 to the south. Three bridges cross the water, the seventeenth-century Sheepwash Bridge near the church distinguished by a stone-walled sheep pen adjoining, used when sheep were dipped in the river. The village is a rather rambling collection of houses, mainly limestone with sandstone dressings, the vernacular idiom still identifiable behind the general tarting up. One three-storey house retains its long weavers' window on the top floor, and the small former tithe-barn has been very tastefully converted into a desirable residence.

Three more examples conveniently complete this survey of limestone villages of the area. Close to Beresford Dale and the High Peak Trail, so beloved of anglers and walkers, Hartington is near the edge of the limestone belt, and this cool grey stone gives cohesive dignity to the houses and inns

Ashford-in-the-Water, Derbyshire. Limestone walls, sandstone dressings

round its large, irregular market place. Buildings are well spaced, many three-storeyed, with round or oval date-panels. Eighteenth-century houses are of limestone, later ones of well-dressed sandstone, mainly with stone-slate or grey slate roofs. A number of small greens break up the metalled area of the centre, one with a small pond, albeit concrete lined. Pretentious façades impose a calm urbanity, and the classical old market hall of 1836 has an arched ground-floor of rusticated masonry, and the early seventeenth-century manor-house is now a youth hostel.

Just over the Staffordshire border Alstonefield has a good variety of houses built of limestone, with sandstone dressings. A network of lanes, two small greens, and a two-tone church unusual in having a chequerboard pattern of masonry, all add up to a vigorous visual informality if not an unduly lively village. It had a market six centuries ago, but soon surrendered any commercial importance to Hartington and Ashbourne, much better placed. To the west is Wetton, breezily isolated above the Manifold Valley, and at the focus of five lanes and as many field paths. Limestone predominates, again with sandstone dressings; seventeenth-century Manor House Farm has low, mullioned windows, but most of the houses and cottages are eighteenth- and nineteenth-century, even the smaller ones having simple flat kneelers terminating the roof-copings. Wetton has the feel of a workaday village, with farms and muddy gateways, stonecrop on the walls, and an integrity which showier villages often lack.

Although the colourful Geological Survey Ten Mile Map shows the pale blue which indicates Carboniferous Limestone to cover a large area of the north Pennines and adjacent parts of Lancashire, limestone villages are not as thick on the ground as they are in Derbyshire, largely because more workable building stones were never far away. However, in the Craven district of the Yorkshire Dales, where the white bones of the landscape so frequently surface as gleaming crags and scars, limestone is used for many buildings, especially in Wharfedale, Littondale and around Malham. Less pliable than gritstone, it could be shaped with a hammer to yield a roughly square lump. From these lumps a rubble wall could be built, but for quoins, lintels, sills, window- and door-openings, sandstone or gritstone was preferred.

Yorkshire's major dales are wider and larger than those of Derbyshire. Settlements and roads are in the valleys, and villages are more nucleated, often round a well-kept green, such as at Linton-in-Craven. A ford, stepping-stones, a clapper bridge, a packhorse bridge and a more modern road bridge span the beck that bisects the green, around which are limestone houses showing a remarkable variety of features yet retaining undoubted harmony. Pride of place goes to Fountaine Hospital, founded and endowed in 1721, unusually distinguished and grand for a small village, with more than a hint of Vanbrughian dignity about its design and the fine ashlared sandstone of its structure. Attractively carved datestones point to seventeenth-century origins

Arncliffe, North Yorkshire. Limestone, rendered on house walls, bare on barns, in one of the most beautiful villages in the Yorkshire Dales. Note how the 30° pitch of stone-slate roofs echoes the slope of the hills beyond

of many of Linton's houses; Georgian fronts have changed their appearance.

In spite of recent additions, Linton's near neighbour, Threshfield, retains its heart around the small triangular remains of a village green with old houses and barns clustered round it. Datestones indicate a wave of prosperity between 1650 and 1675 when the manor-house was built and the grammar school founded – still in use as a primary school. Good porches and stone-mullioned windows are a feature of these seventeenth-century buildings.

Across the river, Grassington is the undoubted capital of upper Wharfedale, its township status centred on an attractive square, cobbled and with just enough trees to create a foil to the shops, inns and houses bordering it. Main Street runs north-eastwards up from the square towards the moor whose lead-mines brought expansion and prosperity to the village in the second half of the eighteenth century. Leading off the square and off Main Street are a number of 'folds', originally small crofts attached to individual houses, but gradually filled in with cottages during the last two centuries. Chapel Fold, Chamber End Fold, Jakey and The Woggins add their own euphonic appeal to the many splendid groups of seventeenth- and eighteenth-century houses, two- and three-storey, mainly of limestone with some of the larger, older houses showing the characteristic local idiom of stepped, tripartite windows in the upper part of a tall porch. One of Grassington's other surprises is the survival of seventeenth-century barns close to the village centre, Platts Barn being an outstanding example, with neatly arched pigeon-holes in the wall of a projecting porch.

Above Grassington, Wharfedale displays limestone scenery to perfection with long scars etching its eastern hillsides between Conistone and Kettlewell and the proud thrust of Kilnsey Crag dominating the main road side of the valley. Beyond Kilnsey, twin minor roads lead up Littondale, where man-made walls of many different periods create their distinctive geometry on valley floor and green hillsides singularly unscarred by either quarrying or lead-mining. Arncliffe is a delightful village, carefully sited on a gravel delta above the flood-plain of the River Skirfare, an Anglian settlement round a spacious green. Seventeenth- and eighteenth-century houses fringe this green, their limestone walling often hidden behind a pale colour-washed rendering. Georgian sash-windows add elegance, but my overriding impression of Arncliffe is the number of farms and their associated barns which are so integral a part of the village scene, more so than in any other Dales village. One barn near the post office is dated 1677. Across the river, past Bridge End where Charles Kingsley visited during his stay at Malham Tarn House, is Old Cotes, dated 1650, one of the most exquisite of houses, with mullioned windows, long roof of sandstone flags, and two-storey porch with tripartite, stepped window. Exciting roads leave Littondale, from Arncliffe to Malham, and from Halton Gill – a hamlet of stone farmhouses – to Stainforth.

Malham lies at the heart of the finest limestone landscapes in Britain. To the

Malham, North Yorkshire. Town Head Farm, one of many late seventeenth- and early eighteenth-century farmhouses in this limestone village in a spectacular limestone landscape. Rubble-stone walls, white-painted sandstone dressings, sandstone roofs

north, Malham Cove is a massive limestone cliff nearly 300ft (91m) high, forming a natural amphitheatre. A mile (1.6km) to the east, waterfalls plunge down the great ravine in the limestone at Gordale Scar. Centuries of settlement and land-use on or near the surface of the fields and hills, stitched by scores of miles of stone walls, are in evidence. In the village, a clear sparkling beck, emerging from the foot of the Cove, divides the few scattered stone cottages, most of them low, simple, often white-washed, mainly of late seventeenth- and early eighteenth-century date, as many date-panels confirm. An early Georgian coaching inn, green verges, stone bridges, Pennine Wayfarers, tourists by the thousand, all make their presence felt in this honeypot of a limestone village in the Dales.

5

Chalk, Flint,
Pebbles and Boulders

Coloured bright green on the Geological Survey Ten Mile Map, the English chalklands lie to the south and east of the oolite, all except a few very tiny pockets near the coast on the Devon–Dorset border. Chalk is one of our youngest and softest limestones and formerly covered almost two-thirds of the country, but wide areas of this have been overlaid with later deposits or have been smothered by the movements of glaciers and their subsequent drift of boulder-clay. Chalk, and the flint so often associated with it, has been widely used as building material over many centuries, but it is rare to find villages where the use of chalk dominates to create the *genius loci* of a particular place.

Chalk's purity as a substance translates into a similar purity in the landscapes it has formed. It is possible to travel from the Dorset coast near Lulworth, northwards and eastwards across Dorset, Wiltshire and Berkshire to the Chilterns, past the Gogmagogs of Cambridgeshire into East Anglia and the north Norfolk coast, and be on the chalk all the way. Then, by leaping across The Wash, the formation can be regained near Skegness and continued north along the Lincolnshire Wolds, and beyond the Humber to the broadening spread of the chalk on the Yorkshire Wolds where it ends abruptly above the broad plain of the Derwent, and on the east meets the North Sea in the shining cliffs at Flamborough and Bempton. Except in its East Anglian section, the chalk has produced a serene, calm landscape of gently swelling uplands which are called downs, with long ridges, protruding spurs, fluted hollows, and clear streams. Chalk country is naturally open country, but has had imposed upon it as clumps, shelter-belts and woodlands – Masefield's 'beech clumps grey that wouldn't be green till the end of May'. But from Beer to Bempton the essence of the chalk is its elemental simplicity, its spaciousness, its imprints of early Man amid the whispering grass, and its appeal to the great English naturalists. Gilbert White, Richard Jefferies and W. H. Hudson are the great singers of its praises.

As a building stone, chalk is very variable. In Kent it is mainly too porous, and in Sussex there are other more serviceable materials. In the western areas it comes into its own, being quite widely used in Dorset, Wiltshire, Hampshire and Berkshire, and less widely so in Bedfordshire, Hertfordshire and

Cambridgeshire. In the wolds of Lincolnshire and Yorkshire occasional chalk cottages are seen, and, as in the other chalk regions, churches are constructed of chalk blocks, but scarcely a whole village. One of its obvious advantages was its softness which made for ease of quarrying and shaping. Squared blocks were easily obtained, but that same softness rendered chalk unsuitable for quoins, jambs, lintels and sills, so for these dressings brick was commonly introduced, or some other durable stone, if one was available.

Because of the ease with which it could be worked, chalk blocks could be evenly coursed and given fine mortar-joints, but it is more common to find it as chalk rubble in cottage walls. After quarrying, it was ideally left for a year or two to dry out and harden, but because of its vulnerability to damp it always had to be given a good base of a tougher material, and walls of chalk needed protection from above by generously overhanging eaves of thatch or tiles. Frequently, a coat of limewash or plaster would be added, with the result that not all chalk-built cottages proclaim at first glance the material used in their construction.

Following the grain of the country from south-west to north-east is as logical for exploring the chalk as for the limestones which are its neighbour to the north for so much of the way, except at the start of the journey. Beer is a particularly attractive fishing village on the East Devon coast, sheltered in its small bay by the great chalk cliffs of Beer Head. Beer Stone is a chalky limestone quarried since Roman times, but with its greatest period of use during the fifteenth and sixteenth centuries when so many Devon churches

Ashbury, Oxfordshire. Chalk blocks, brick surrounds, wooden lintels, 'S' strengthening bars; and a fine thatched roof

were being enlarged or completely rebuilt. Mined by adit from underground rather than by surface extraction, the stone continued to be worked until well into this century, and a number of houses in the main street of Beer are built of it, including 'The Cottage' at the bottom of the street, thatched, three-storey, with squared chalk quoins but wooden lintels and surrounds to openings.

One of the best areas in which to see the extent – and even here it is limited – to which chalk has been used as a building stone in villages and hamlets is along the foot of the northern escarpment of the Marlborough Downs and the Berkshire Downs. Compton Bassett, near Calne, has a number of chalk cottages, mainly whitewashed and thatched, with deep overhangs, while to the east of Swindon, on the edge of the Vale of White Horse, Bishopstone, Idstone and Ashbury continue the theme. Bishopstone has some attractive groups of chalk cottages, some with brick dressings, some with stone surrounds and quoins. Roofing materials are equally varied, thatch or clay tile, so that there is no marked degree of unity. Plaster and whitewash disguise some of the chalk, and the occasional use of chalk gives a mottled appearance to the church. Idstone is little more than a hamlet of farms and a few cottages, all of chalk with brick dressings, but standing very much as individuals rather than as groups. Golden lichen colours tile roofs; lanes and paths lead into the fields beyond. Ashbury is larger, with a few groups of chalk cottages, but these are outnumbered by those constructed of brownish flints, or of more recent brick.

Uffington, as seems appropriate to a village which has given its name to the most venerable of Britain's hill figures of the chalk, is probably the best of the chalk villages. Six lanes converge on this large, sprawling place which spreads itself rather untidily in the form of a huge oval a mile (1.6km) round, with not a nucleus in sight, unless it is the corner by the octagonal-towered church and the little school nearby. This is one of Uffington's most satisfying buildings, resembling a tiny barn, of good blocks of chalk on a stout plinth of large sarsen stones. A neat roundel above the rear door carries a date-plaque of 1611, and the tiled roof shows a colourful invasion of lichen. Chalk cottages, with some larger ones such as Dragon House with two storeys within the steeply thatched roof space, are scattered round the village. Generally, the chalk is roughly coursed, usually with largest blocks in the lower part of walls graded to smaller pieces higher up. Brick dressings are commonplace, and occasionally brick relieving arches are introduced. Nineteenth-century cottages use very small chalk blocks in their walls, no bigger than bricks, and throughout the village thatch and clay tiles are the roofing materials.

A harder type of chalk containing marl, and generally known as clunch, occurs around Dunstable, where it has been quarried since medieval times. Although used in some churches in the area it does not contribute markedly to the appearance and character of villages, not even Totternhoe where the most famous quarries were situated. To the north-east, the Cambridgeshire

Uffington, Oxfordshire. The Jacobean Old School House of large chalk blocks shows the use of a good hard stone base for this soft building stone

landscape shows few of the usual characteristics of chalk country, and although Burwell, Swaffham Bulbeck and Swaffham Prior are quoted as villages where chalk has commonly been used as a building stone, you need to walk around the back lanes to see any surviving evidence. Burwell's street extends for a couple of miles and almost all the buildings have been faced with brick, and not very attractive brick at that, from local gault-clay brickworks. Occasionally, colour-washed walls of gables and the backs of houses probably hide chalk rubble, while at Swaffham Bulbeck a good, chalk-built barn is a reminder of what once was, but otherwise only the scars of many small chalk-pits remain of the source of a former widely used stone.

The chalk does not reappear as an important landscape feature until north of The Wash, where it forms the gently swelling uplands of the Lincolnshire Wolds. In times past it is likely that wolds villages would have had a fair number of chalk buildings, but it is difficult to find many examples today because stucco and plaster hide the original chalk rubble or the neglect of earlier centuries has resulted in a complete rebuilding. One or two rather tatty chalk cottages do survive at Swaby, where, as is common throughout the wolds, pantiles are used on roofs.

Beyond the Humber and the county to which the river has given its name, the wold landscape continues, more open and spacious than in Lincolnshire,

89

the chalk itself is harder, and, unlike the downland variety of southern England, contains no flints. However, the presence of a good limestone not far away to the west, together with the development of a flourishing brick-making industry around Hull and Beverley since medieval times, has resulted in a dearth of the use of chalk as a building stone. Almost the only villages where it has been used for more than the occasional cottage or barn are on the coast north of Bridlington. Flamborough Head is the greatest promontory on the east coast, where the northern arc of the chalk wolds swings round and juts 5 miles (8km) into the North Sea. Flamborough village lies 2 miles (3.2km) inland from the cave-riddled cliffs, a sprawling place where sufficient numbers of eighteenth- and nineteenth-century houses survive among the modern additions to allow the village to have a memory. Very few houses, however, are of chalk, and these have the usual arrangement of brick for quoins and dressings.

Bempton, to the north, is more compact; a crowded cluster of cottages in narrow streets, mainly of brick, but with chalk in evidence near the green. Nearby, Speeton is smaller, very rural, with occasional glimpses of chalk in a few buildings which, if nothing else, can probably claim to be the northernmost examples in Britain of the use of chalk as a building stone.

Easington, Humberside. Shore-cobbles in decorative herring-bone pattern, with plenty of mortar. White-painted woodwork enhances

To the south of Bridlington is the alluvial plain of Holderness, culminating in the appendix projection of Spurn Head into the mouth of the Humber. Glacial drift and boulder-clay deposited over Holderness huge numbers of rounded cobbles, stones derived from a great variety of rocks and scattered over the fields. Obviously anxious to be rid of them, farmers used them as building stones, and they were even used for church building. Shore-cobbles, too, were convenient, and a number of villages in the southern part of Holderness show the use of these attractive rounded stones in domestic and farm buildings, Easington being a particularly good example. A mile (1.6km) from the Humber and less than that from the crumbling North Sea coast, it is a place of sea breezes and clean fresh air. Its church tower rises above the bright pantiled roofs of the village with its broad open street leading to the east, a narrow winding one to the south. From the tower arch the 'Easington Imp' looks grotesquely down, and two windows in the north aisle have medieval gravestones as lintels. But much of the church itself, as well as many cottage walls and the boundary walls of fields around the village, are constructed of shore-cobbles, laid in herring-bone patterns, creating an attractive if 'busy' appearance, better appreciated in a small barn near the church, where a greater wall area heightens the effects, although this is partially over-shadowed by a fine, brick-built tithe-barn nearby with a splendid thatched roof. There is thatch, too, at Skeffling, a small village south of the road that leads westwards through these low-lying landscapes on the edge of Holderness, where cobbles in the walls are a constant reminder that the sea is never far away.

Rounded cobbles from the shore and the fields used in buildings north of the Humber are usually quite large. Obviously, in order to maintain roughly level courses, it was necessary to choose stones of similar size, and although they may have come from different types of parent rock, they have the common factor of having been carried by glacier ice or water and in the process have become generally rounded. Their shape made it essential that each cobble and each course of cobbles should be well embedded in mortar to ensure stability. Yet the surprising thing about cobble walls is that the mortared joints are relatively inconspicuous, having been set well back from the wall face. This effect is even more marked where flint cobbles have been used for buildings, which is the case in East Anglia. Here it is necessary to distinguish between cobbles and pebbles, and, according to Mr Alec Clifton-Taylor, the distinction is one of size only, with pebbles being not more than 3in (76mm) in diameter and cobbles varying in size greater than this. Over large areas of Norfolk, parts of Suffolk and Essex, flint is the principal building material, often rough, unbroken flints from fields, but nearer the coast, flint pebbles from the beach are used.

Of all our building stones, flint has probably the longest known use, and no other country has employed it to the extent that England has done. Its geological origins are uncertain, its structure peculiar, its qualities unique. So hard as to be virtually indestructible by normal weathering processes, it can yet be fractured quite easily in any plane. When fresh it is almost black, usually with a white chalky covering acquired through its long association with the chalk in which it naturally occurs. Where this chalk meets the sea, as along the north-west coast of Norfolk, water and wave erosion, over the centuries, have loosened the chalky matrix to dislodge the pebbles of flint within it and gradually rolled them around on the shore, smoothing their surfaces and making them desirable building material in an area lacking any others.

Thus, a journey along that most hauntingly beautiful coast eastwards from Hunstanton to Cromer, by the curiously winding A149 which Dr Hoskins suggests follows the line of a medieval route from village to village, which itself evolved from the winding tracks trampled out by cattle as they were driven each day to and from the marshes, leads through a series of villages where flint cottages abound. Sand-dunes, saltings, tidal creeks where sea-lavender flourishes, small natural harbours, silted-up estuaries and towering skies give this coast a windy, shining splendour unsurpassed in Britain. Under the right weather conditions, usually with a cool breeze blowing in from the Wash, Norfolk light has its own magic quality, imposing a startling brilliance to the colours and textures of tile, flint and brick. Flint always needs the squared solidity of brick (or stone) to give essential rigidity to walls, for rounded flint pebbles used in courses, or knapped flints with almost square, flat faces, need to be ringed with, and laid in, thick layers of mortar. Since such layers required time to dry, only small amounts of walling could be done at any one time. As a result, flint walls tended to bulge, and to overcome this not only brick quoins, jambs, window-openings and eaves were necessary, but it was often an advantage to introduce strengthening 'lacing' or string courses of brick laid horizontally, and often in decorative pattern, every few feet along the walls. This was particularly so where small flints had been used.

Shallow segmental brick arches above lower windows, sometimes above doors, provide a contrast in line; chimney-stacks are invariably brick, and pantile roofs, especially on older houses where they have replaced thatch, are quite steeply pitched, about 50°, mainly gabled. Many cottages have pantiled dormers whose roof slope is less than that of the main roof, so most north

Flint faced walls

Brancaster, Norfolk. Flint and brick terraces. Note the windows almost flush with wall faces, and characteristic eastern-counties pantile roofs

Norfolk villages are strongly two-toned in their harmony – warm reds and pinks of brick and pantile, cool greys of broken flints in their walls, all highlighted by wooden windows and door-frames, white-painted and set well forward so that they are flush with the brickwork of the jamb, not recessed as is more normal. While this obviously gives good interior window-sills, it also means that the wooden frames are less protected from the wind and weather, and eliminates what is often a very pleasant pattern of light and shade created by recessed frames.

From Holme-next-the-Sea to Cley, over 20 miles (32km) eastwards the sea is separated from the A149 by wide sands, saltings and salt marsh, with natural bays protected by sand-dunes. As far as Overy Staithe small villages are spaced very regularly at 2 mile (3.2km) intervals, the first ones, Thornham and Titchwell showing more chalk than flint, being near the edge of a narrow belt of stone that reaches northwards from Downham Market. Brancaster, growing on golf and sailing, has one good street, a gentle curve of flint-walled houses, brick-dressed, and with occasional chalk gables. Along the road, Brancaster Staithe's cottages show lively variety in materials – flint, chalk, carstone and brick. Flinty gables face the road; coursed flint pebbles with brick dressings and decoration catch the sunlight and glow; white woodwork gleams.

By the time the Burnhams are reached brick predominates, yet a few miles south by the B1355, North and South Creake redress the balance. Each has a good proportion of flint cottages, more noticeably grouped or terraced at

93

Blakeney

North Creake, where flint has been used in a number of new houses, although the old forge is a chalk building. A few miles eastwards beyond the valley of the River Stiffkey, Binham is close-clustered and compact, characteristically built round two or three large farmsteads in a wide, empty landscape. Flint is everywhere, on house walls, barns and outbuildings, even in the walls of the sadly truncated priory west of the village, although stone has been used for dressings and buttresses.

Blakeney lays fair claim to be the most beautiful village in Norfolk, no small thanks to the far-sightedness of a local housing society which pioneered the restoration of old cottages which had deteriorated during World War II. Dozens of houses were saved, given a new lease of life, and let initially to local people. Since then, commuters and second-homers have moved in, and spruce and select flint-and-brick cottages along the High Street, or huddled round cosy courtyards, reflect the care and attention lavished on them.

Further along the coast, Cley (it rhymes with 'sky'), has been a mile (1.6km) inland since reclamation left it there in the seventeenth century. Lacking the sailing ethos which permeates Blakeney, it compensates by having a fine windmill converted into a private house, an eighteenth-century customs house, shining flint-and-brick cottages, and a haunting seaward landscape of marshes and mudflats, gullies and creeks, and soaring skies. Some 2 miles (3.2km) away, Salthouse, too, has flint pebbles in the walls of its houses, many of which required rebuilding after the great tidal surges of 1953.

Suffolk's flint villages are around Breckland, mainly to the south-west of Thetford. Icklingham shows the use of a very dark grey flint in association with grey bricks for dressings, producing a sombre appearance relieved in some cases by the use of lighter, multi-coloured flints in gables. Eriswell, a few miles north-west, has an impressive row of seven early Victorian cottages, one-up, one-down, with a particularly flinty Chequers Inn beyond.

Although flint occurs in association with the chalk whose swelling downlands extend over so many miles of southern England, there are no villages where it has been used exclusively. Churches, castles, farms and barns, individual houses and cottages have all been built with this difficult stone, but nowhere does it impart a distinct ethos to a particular village as it does in north Norfolk. If I had to choose a representative from the chalk counties I should plump for Hambleden in Buckinghamshire, reached by curling roads from the gentle hills meeting at a small triangular green graced by a chestnut. True, there are brick cottages and some half-timbering, but there are rows of flint-and-brick, with clay-tile roofs, a church tower of flint, and a sufficient shininess of knapped flint walls to give an echo of East Anglia.

Dorset's chalk belt, covering almost half the county, is sparsely populated, and flint is widely used, particularly in the central area, but always mixed with other materials. At Sydling St Nicholas, secretively situated in the gentle valley of the Sydling Water, thatched cottages spaced out along the gently curving High Street have walls showing flint and stone used decoratively in alternate broad bands, an idiom seen in other chalk-stream villages in both

Hambleden, Buckinghamshire. Flint and brick, mainly of 1871 estate building, with cobbles at the front

Dorset and Wiltshire. Two or three larger houses of the seventeenth and early eighteenth centuries display the same treatment, but an older tithe-barn has flint walls and stone buttresses, and, unfortunately, a corrugated iron roof. Above the village the Sydling Water appears to emerge from a series of ponds below the encircling downs, but later in its brief journey to join the Frome a few miles from Dorchester it shows the happy chalk-stream habit of doing occasional vanishing tricks.

Banded stone and flint seems to be rather more common in Dorset than in Wiltshire, where chequerwork more often prevails, particularly towards the east. A number of quiet villages strung out along the chalk rivers which gentle their ways from the grey plain have cottages of flint and stone, or flint and brick, noticeably at Great Wishford and the trio of Langfords in the Wylye valley. But perhaps the most unexpected building stone of Wiltshire's chalk is, geologically, its newest, the sarsen stone, a hard grey sandstone that once covered the chalk. Being a sandstone it conveniently leads to the next chapter.

Cley

6

Sandstone Villages
of Vales and Downs

Sandstone shares with limestone and chalk the basic characteristics of having been deposited in water and built up through the ages in layers. Such sedimentary rocks are usually stratified, with some layers producing better building stones than others. Unlike limestone, most of which was organic in origin, sandstone is purely a mineral rock, consisting mainly of quartz particles, often associated with small amounts of other minerals, chiefly mica and felspar, less frequently with organic remains like shell fragments, the whole cemented by a matrix whose varied character determines the nature of the sandstone. Whereas quartz is almost indestructible, the matrix is vulnerable to erosion, and since many sandstones are not always uniform in composition they have created unexpected problems when used for building.

Sandstone never had the life which lay at the limestone's heart, but its varied mineral content has given it a greater range of colour, through the gamut of greys and buffs to pale yellows and chocolate browns, from a delicate lavender through a blush of pinks and reds to greens and purples. The time-spread of sandstones is similarly wide-ranging, with each geological system being represented. However, over much of the southern half of England where sandstones do occur, other building materials have been more easily available, and it is unusual to find whole villages whose ethos depends on it. Except for those of Cretaceous times, the sandstones are older than the limestones, and therefore make their appearance to the north and west of the Jurassic belt, and it is usually these older ones which seem to show the greatest colour variation.

Paradoxically, however, it is the newest sandstones which provide our oldest man-made structures. Sarsens are boulders of siliceous sandstone lying on the surface of the chalk downs, especially in Wiltshire, hard fragments surviving from a layer that formerly covered the surface, worn by wind, water and frost, and thus eminently suitable to be used by Bronze Age builders for their megalithic temples at Avebury and Stonehenge.

Only about a quarter of Avebury's great stones survive. The remainder have been broken into small lumps and used in building some of the houses in the village and barns nearby. This is not sufficient, however, to justify calling

Avebury a sarsen village, but enough to make it a unique one. Further north, below the edge of the chalk, Bishopstone, Ashbury and Idstone show sarsens in some house walls, but less impressively than at Avebury.

Far more widespread than the eccentric sarsens are the greensands, occurring along the southern edge of the North Downs from east Kent to Selborne in Hampshire, and swinging back as a narrow bench along the northern foot of the South Downs from Petersfield to Eastbourne. Again, however, although it can be identified in individual buildings, it was not used extensively or exclusively. Around Midhurst are a few villages where almost a third of the houses are of sandstone – Rogate, Woolbeding, Amberley and Bury – usually with brick dressings, but the most attractive groupings of sandstone cottages in the chalk country of the south are on the Isle of Wight. Winkle Street at Calbourne benefits from its cul-de-sac quality and necessary pedestrian approach past a flint-faced polygonal gatehouse. Across the clear Caul Bourne and its watercress beds, eighteenth-century thatched or tiled cottages vie with an equally attractive group at Godshill, while Shorwell and Brighstone also show good examples of rubble-stone building.

The Geological Survey Ten Mile Map shows another narrow belt of greensand following the familiar orientation across the country from East Devon and Dorset, gradually swinging away from the Jurassic line through

Avebury, Wiltshire. Sarsen stone, broken into roughly square blocks

West Newton, Norfolk. On the Sandringham estate: dark carstone, used in very small pieces, with dressings and decoration in pale brick

Bedfordshire and Cambridgeshire to north-west Norfolk. Because in most of these areas better stones are available, it is not until Norfolk, where it is the only building stone apart from flint, that its use is sufficiently widespread to result in a few villages showing it almost exclusively. By now impregnated with iron oxide to give it a markedly brown colour, and hence its Norfolk description as 'gingerbread stone', its coarse gritty structure gives it the name carstone.

Keeping to the east of the Great Ouse, as it idles its northward way to King's Lynn, the A10 passes through, or close to, Norfolk's carstone villages where the stone can so easily be mistaken for small dark bricks. The church at Denver and a number of houses near it show this aspect in neatly coursed walls, and Stow Bardolph continues the idiom, though with more use of brick as dressings in estate housing west of the main road. North Runcton, a mile (1.6km) from the A10, has several good houses of carstone, using it also in larger blocks in the church and school, while a barn behind the school shows galletting, a decorative treatment of the white, chalk-based mortar in which are placed small fragments of carstone like rows of nail-heads.

Estate housing around Sandringham, particularly at West Newton dating from early this century, shows random walling of slate-thin carstone with no visible mortar, pale brick dressings above and around windows, and triangular

99

gables. The principal carstone quarries were at Snettisham a few miles up the road, so it is not surprising that most houses here are of carstone, some with their brick dressings picked out in white to relieve the dark, gloomy appearance of the stone under dull, grey skies. Ingoldisthorpe looks distinctly prettier, while Hunstanton Road at Heacham has a row of gabled houses and a shorter 1827 terrace opposite, all of this Norfolk speciality. But perhaps because the carstone cottages at Wereham, east of Downham Market, are mixed in with some of flint and brick, and some colour-wash, giving lively visual and textural contrast, I found this village particularly appealing. Or perhaps it was its good, well-kept pond with well-fed geese and ducks.

Ducks, too, add life and character to the fine pond at East Quantoxhead, reached by narrow, winding, high-hedged lanes at the wooded northern end of the Quantocks. Sandstone is a predominant rock over this western part of Somerset, responsible for the impressive upland scenery not only of the Quantocks but also for the Brendons and the wide moors and wooded combes of Exmoor. Other building materials, especially cob, are very widespread so that very few villages are wholly built of stone. Rubble-walled cottages at East Quantoxhead are loosely dispersed near the pond, their walls purple-brown or grey as in the superb range of pantiled stables, cowsheds and a noble barn near the church. A terrace of four small cottages near the pond has single slabs of lichened slate above their doors, and always there is the view to the friendly hills.

Bishop's Lydeard, Somerset. Warm pink-brown random sandstone, in walls and quoins, in High Street

Sheltered by trees, close-clustered around its church, Bicknoller's houses are of warm red sandstone, sometimes colour-washed, some thatched, some pantiled. A few miles away Crowcombe is mainly colour-washed, and what naked stone exists is markedly greyer, although the beautiful church and the church house opposite redress the colour balance. Cothelstone is little more than a large Jacobean manor, dusky-pink, with white limestone dressings and flourishes of finials, but Bishop's Lydeard, bypassed by the busy Taunton road, has a noble church of warm red stone, with window tracery picked out in golden Ham stone. Houses in High Street east of the church are all built of random red sandstone, their white woodwork a stark, clean contrast. Almshouses nearby of 1854 merely use the stone as dressings, but elsewhere in the village modern development is characteristically tasteless.

Stogumber's rising main street shows pink sandstone only occasionally on gable walls, most frontages being obscured by plaster and whitewash, an idiom repeated at Monksilver below the Brendons' eastern slope. Treborough and Luxborough, however, nearer the crest of the hills, have grey-brown slaty sandstone unadorned, some walls with slate-hanging, the slates for this and for roofs having been brought across the Bristol Channel from Wales.

Although white or colour-washed cob, with deep thatch, create coy charm in many villages west of Minehead, Allerford retains a memorable group of robust red sandstone houses, round-chimneyed and pantiled beyond a narrow, two-arched packhorse bridge with a rich green backcloth of the wooded slopes of Selworthy Beacon. Naked stone survives, too, at Porlock Weir, where more pantiled roofs are a colourful reminder that, outside the eastern counties, Bridgwater was the most important centre for the manufacture of pantiles from the end of the eighteenth century, a result of the influence of its trade with Holland. The use of pantiles spread outwards from Bridgwater, extending sometimes beyond the borders of Somerset.

The county's western neighbour can well be thought of as *the* sandstone county of England, but the rock gives its bright, glowing colour to the soil rather than to the settlements. Of the whole series of sandstones collectively called Devonian, it is the Old Red Sandstone which is responsible for the northern moors as well as for the South Hams. The Culm Measure sandstones cover most of Devon between the moors but are used as building material only in small, hard, rubbly pieces. The New Red Sandstone of Triassic times runs down the eastern edge of the county, culminating in the colourful cliffs by Dawlish and Teignmouth, yet there is no single village whose character is visually determined by the beauty of bare stone. However, before leaving the south and west it is worth a slight detour into Dorset again, to Chideock, between Lyme Regis and Bridport. A mile (1.6km) to the south-west, Golden Cap is the highest cliff on the south coast, so named from the rich colour of its flat summit plateau, a sandstone used for most of the cottages along both sides of Chideock's busy main street. Smooth-faced blocks, mullioned windows, white woodwork, thatch or slate roofs occur repeatedly in this linear village of warm, yellow-buff stone.

The Old Red Sandstone gives to Herefordshire its fine red soils and the grey-pink tones of its churches and major houses. But half-timbering is more the rule for villages, where use of the stone is restricted to footings and foundations. In the southern half of Shropshire the Old Red is associated with many other rocks, some much older, so that a journey across the county from, say, Cleobury Mortimer to Welshpool, crosses most of these formations. But in such a journey you would be more likely to remember the views than the villages, where stone occurs only intermittently.

In the vale country on each side of Wenlock's wooded limestone crest, quiet places have roots deep in the past. Diddlebury is Corvedale's largest parish, and the circular churchyard is evidence of great antiquity. A poplar-lined approach from the B4368 leads to a wide, shallow stream near the church, a farmhouse and nearby cottages in yellow or pink stone loosely grouped, and a gentle hill climbing past the village school. Nearby, Munslow mixes half-timbering with its buff stone, but across the hills, beyond Rushbury, Cardington is far more rewarding. Sheltering beneath a semi-circle of distinctive hills, The Lawley, Caer Caradoc and Cardington Hill, stone houses cluster round the trees and tower of the parish church. Neat rows of dormered cottages, some fronted by stone-walled gardens, lead to good groups of farm buildings; the Royal Oak has whitened its stone, although without wholly disguising it.

The New Red Sandstone extends from the west Midlands, creating low-lying fertile vales from Nottinghamshire to south-east Durham, and, more importantly for stone villages, to Furness and the Cumbrian coast, reappearing inland as an elongated limb from near Carlisle to Kirkby Stephen. Pastoral landscapes carpet the Vale of Eden between the mountains of eastern Lakeland and the high, lonely Pennines to the east, and among a score of compact villages Temple Sowerby, a few miles north of Appleby, shows more than most the beauty of bare red stone. A small green separates the A66 from the best houses to its east, which glow almost crimson in evening sunlight. Even the few brick infillers achieve a remarkable match. At Kirkby Thore, to the south, more humble houses tend to be colour-washed but keep red sandstone dressings, while Morland, one of a number of delightful villages near the Lyvennet valley, enjoys its own clear stream, a ford and tiny bridges, and white-painted low houses along its banks.

Most of the best villages lie between the A66 and the Pennines. At Long Marton long front gardens grace houses whose walls of red sandstone have very thin mortar courses. Colour-wash is rare so the impression is of massive strength and dignity. Dufton, 2 miles (3.2km) away, presents a different picture, its broad green with an avenue of trees and late eighteenth-century cottages and farms down each side. Walls are white or colour-washed, with

Dufton

dressings of red stone left bare. A late Georgian pump is painted maroon, a favourite colour here, and always, to the east, is the superb backcloth of Dufton Pike's shapely cone.

A few miles north-west, Milburn is outstanding, a perfect example of the many nucleated villages consistently situated along the 600ft (183m) contour below the Pennine escarpment. Stone houses, cottages and farms are grouped round all sides of a long rectangular green sloping slightly down from east to west where the view opens across the vale. Narrow paths between houses giving access to farm buildings behind are the only breaks in the almost continuous frontage of eighteenth- and nineteenth-century houses which represent a quite late rebuilding. Although a number of houses are colour-washed, sufficient bare stone remains, which, with the stone dressings either left bare or painted maroon, ensures that Milburn merits inclusion.

Newbiggin, Blencarn, Skirwith and Ousby are little more than stone hamlets, but Great Salkeld, by the west bank of the Eden 6 miles (10km) north-east of Penrith, is another particularly good village of red sandstone houses. Unusually, the stone has been dressed into small blocks so that at first sight it may be mistaken for bricks. However, the quality is undeniable, with very little colour-wash or rendering, and this linear village provides a nice contrast with Milburn, while its church tower was built as a pele, tunnel-vaulted with tall narrow slits for windows, a late fourteenth-century defence against marauding Scots.

At Kirkoswald, a few miles to the north, the church has even stranger distinctions. A holy spring issues from near its west front at the foot of a hill, and the church tower is 200yd (61m) away, a hilltop campanile built in 1897

103

to replace an older wooden structure. The village is also on a hill and climbs even higher to the north, a place of beautiful red stone, some colour-washed but most left bare. Cobbles give colour and texture to pavements and a small square graced by eighteenth-century houses. Roofs are stone or slate, some paths are of red sandstone flags, and the local folk really care about their village whose finest building is the college, founded in 1523 and dissolved in 1547, since when the Featherstonehaugh family have lived there, although the ornate red sandstone entrance and main elevation of the house are late seventeenth century.

One of England's most unusual sandstones is almost wholly responsible for the fine landscapes and buildings of the North Yorkshire Moors National Park. While it is Jurassic limestones which impart character and unique charm to the Cotswolds, and are quarried at a few places in north-east Yorkshire, it is Jurassic sandstones that provide a superb building material in the very beautiful region of sweeping heather moors intersected by sheltered fertile dales behind Helmsley, Pickering, Scarborough and Whitby, and including the Cleveland and Hambleton Hills. Most of the stone is fine textured, varying in colour from rich gold to light brown, buff and grey-brown, and, used in conjunction with bright pink pantiles as the chief roofing material, with a certain amount of Welsh slate, and almost invariably white-painted woodwork, produces the most colourful villages in England. Only rarely is the stone itself painted, but left natural, used in regular courses with larger hewn blocks for lintels and dressings. The area has never been particularly wealthy so that most houses and farms are modest in size. Quarrying and mineral-working of eighteenth- and nineteenth-century times has resulted in many villages having short terraces or small groups of cottages, contrasting with the farmhouses either isolated or in villages, two-storeyed and with barns or byres added at one end but lower than the house. Thus, roof lines are discontinuous, and, viewed along a street, present a pleasing rhythm of gables or part-gables.

Gables frequently have copings with kneelers – projecting stone brackets that end gable parapets at the eaves, as though to allay the impression that the coping-stones would slide off – and are very rarely hipped. Thus, there is a clean simplicity of line, which, with front walls whose area of masonry is much greater than that of the windows, creates a remarkably calm quality which makes the villages of this region so satisfying.

(opposite)

Kirkoswald, Cumbria. Pink sandstone, ashlared, on the left; painted window surrounds beyond; white-painted stone on the right. Cobbles, flags also of sandstone, roofs of stone-slate flags. Curving, descending main street offers a succession of attractive vistas and groups

Milburn, Cumbria. Broad rectangular green, closed at the upper end, with the Pennines beyond. Pink sandstone, some colour-wash and some window surrounds painted. The maypole is a focal point

Osmotherley, North Yorkshire. Dark yellow sandstone, pink pantile and white paint, all within a few miles of Teesside

Osmotherley, on a shelf below the western escarpment of the Hambleton Hills, is as warm and rewarding as its name implies. North Street, South Street and West End meet at the village centre, a market cross and stone table, where the southwards view leads the eye past houses of grey-brown stone to distant hills. Cobbled pavements front the Three Tuns and the Queen Catherine and in North Street tree-lined grass verges form a different foil for dark stone and pink pantile. Nothing jars. Behind the village are the moors, with an inviting, exciting road climbing past Chequers, a former drovers' inn, to Hawnby and Ryedale, while for walkers the greater challenge is the famous Lyke Wake Walk, a 40 mile (64km) endurance route starting from Osmotherley, heading along the crest of the Cleveland Hills and crossing the heart of the moorland plateau to finish on the coast at Ravenscar.

Had the terminus been 2 miles (3.2km) to the north, the walk would have linked two of the best stone villages, for Robin Hood's Bay is unforgettable, once you've passed the rather ordinary streets at the top of its sea-seeking hill. The main street, from which visitors' cars should be excluded, twists down the cliff, past a tumble of roofs and gables. Tightly packed cottages, shops and chapels line the road, and narrow alleys, passages and steps thread cobbled ways on each side, by stone walls, cute porches, white-framed windows, and even a few miniscule gardens. Close-up cameos exclude the sky, so you are

106

made aware more than in most villages of
the compelling presence of stone, and the
ingenuity with which it has been packed
and parcelled into stepped sequences of
houses from the sea-wall, seemingly to the
sky.

Staithes, another close-knit village to
the north of Whitby, has similar if less
dramatic qualities, being concentrated
nearer to the foot of a hill, seen very well
from across the cleft of Roxby Beck which
provides a tiny anchorage for boats.

If the coastal villages are close-clustered,
those of the moors have space. Goathland, a
few miles south-west of Whitby, spreads
itself generously around a series of broad,
sheep-cropped greens. Grey stone houses
are at the moor's edge, with space before
them, space between and space beyond.

Robin Hoods Bay

Only in the road near the station is there any sign of compactness by terracing;
even the squat-towered Art Nouveau church of late Victorian times is tucked
on at the southern end of the village. All around is the powerful presence of the
sombre moors with their manifold prehistoric remains, while the present
asserts its fantasy in the view of the Fylingdales radomes from the Pickering
road to the south.

Robin Hoods Bay

My boyhood holidays in the early 1930s were spent at Whitby, reached then by train from Teesside as, indeed, it still can be, along the Esk Valley line. I have never forgotten the roll-call team of stations – Kildale, Commondale, Castleton, Danby, Lealholm, Glaisdale, Egton, Grosmont, Sleights, Ruswarp, Whitby. There is still no easy road-route down the valley, for the villages are linked haphazardly by minor roads and lanes. But for views as well as villages 10 miles (16km) in Eskdale offers as good rewards as anywhere in England, with stone and pantile dominant. Castleton straggles up its hill on the southern side of the valley, and Danby does the same on the opposite bank a couple of miles down dale. Sheep graze the green at Danby End, and again at Lealholm, much nearer the river. Grey-stone Glaisdale spreads itself on the southern hillside, and tortuous lanes writhe from the valley bottom in a circuitous route to Egton – twin villages, one on the windy crest to the north where five lanes meet, and its valley partner by the river, the station, the Catholic church and its schoolroom where, on the first Tuesday in every August, is held the famous show organised by the Egton Bridge Old Gooseberry Society (founded in 1800). While the major prize is for the heaviest gooseberry – the best this century being nearly 2oz (57g) – the most impressive display is usually that of a twelve-berry group, probably weighing in at over 1lb (454g).

Woods and hedgerows give the north-east dales a more pastoral appearance than their Pennine counterparts, but stone walls pattern the hillsides and accompany many roads and tracks. Massive stone gateposts are testimony to the ease with which the bedrock was quarried and worked, and you cannot travel far without seeing small, abandoned quarries. Many miles of stone-flagged causeways cross the open moors, packhorse routes, monks' trods, salters' ways, fishways, and a score of lonely crosses or guideposts suggest many moorland journeyings in times past.

Two of the most famous of these, Ralph Cross and Fat Betty, are on the high moors crossed by the north–south road from Castleton to Hutton-le-Hole, showplace of all the moorland villages. A beck chuckles down the centre of a long, uneven green, crossed by white wooden footbridges. Well-spaced houses of mellow stone, each gay-gardened, loosely line the roads up each side, many of them dating back to the late seventeenth century when Quakerism flourished here. Four centuries of local life are evoked in the exhibits at the Ryedale Folk Museum, next to the Crown Inn, but when the summer and Sunday crowds have left, the stone harmonies of Hutton survive in a relieved quiet, no longer competing with shiny metal.

(opposite)————————————————————————————————

Robin Hood's Bay, North Yorkshire. Warm yellow sandstone, pink pantile: point and counterpoint. A gem of colours, textures, angles and gables

Danby, North Yorkshire. Roof line and window rhythm in this village of the moors

Nearby, Lastingham has far deeper roots, a church founded in Saxon times and with a rare, surviving Norman crypt. Dignified houses of grey stone are loosely grouped around the church, along the street past a memorial well, with cottages by a stream. No ostentation here, but perhaps more sanctity in the stone, and you have a splendid view of the village set against its moorland backcloth from Spaunton Bank immediately to the south.

The busy Helmsley–Scarborough road, the A170, bypasses a number of villages, but near Helmsley and a mile (1.6km) to the north of the road, Pockley deserves a visit because six of its pale stone houses retain their thatched roofs. Indeed, the steep pitch of these suggests that they once covered cruck-framed structures. White wooden window-frames and lintels contrast well with stone and thatch, and the single street shows separate cottages and farms throughout its length, the linear appearance enhanced by the long, low, single-storey buildings. Where thatch has not been used roofs have been pantiled.

Single-storey, sandstone and pantile characterise Northumberland's nucleated, but widely scattered villages north of the Tyne. Although limestone is present, it is scarcely used for building, but Fell Sandstones, fine gritstones and sandstones from the coal measures have yielded good building stones, so that, away from the industrial corner in the south-east, and elsewhere, apart from recent housing estates, Northumberland is a county of sandstone buildings. Its troubled past as a Border county and subsequent late settled development have brought about a simple austerity of domestic architecture to which the grey or grey-brown sandstone seems entirely suited.

A few miles west of Newcastle, and almost too close for comfort, Stamfordham appears to be a perfect example of a northern green-village, but is really an unusual piece of co-operative eighteenth-century planning. An enclosure award of 1735 decreed that the joint owners, Sir John Swinburne of Capheaton, and Balliol College, Oxford, should enjoy rights on the green, together with their tenants and farmers and villagers whose houses were built around the green. The result is a particularly harmonious estate village, more in stone than brick, together with a covered village cross, a neat lock-up, and a pound.

Villages are in the river valleys of North Tyne, Rede, Wansbeck, Aln and Coquet, together with a handful of coastal settlements. North of Hexham but south of the Roman Wall and lying just off the Corn Road, the village of Wall nestles beneath a whin-covered hillside. Church, reading-room and two or three houses occupy an island site at the centre of a rectangular green, with grey stone cottages, slate-roofed, surrounding it.

Bellingham (pronounced Bellinjum) is the old capital of the North Tyne, now the gateway to the new landscapes of forest and reservoir around Kielder. Yet in the middle of last century it was the centre of an iron industry which provided some of the material used in Stephenson's great High Level Bridge

Stamfordham, Northumberland. Eighteenth-century planned village with a large green and variety of grey-buff stone houses

across the Tyne at Newcastle. Most village buildings in grey-brown stone reflect that industrial element, with a short, wide main street, a market place at slightly lower level flanked by sturdy houses, pubs, shops and a nineteenth-century town hall with clock-tower. Compactness characterises this friendly village, last shopping-place for northbound Pennine Wayfarers, and scene of one of the Border county's great agricultural shows which has developed from the former annual wool fair. Following three centuries of Border strife when it was so frequently fired, the twelfth-century parish church of St Cuthbert was rebuilt in the early seventeenth century with a barrel-vaulted roof of huge stone slabs spanning twenty-two arches, massively medieval in idiom, and manifestly fire-proof.

Clouds drift north-eastwards across Northumberland's windy uplands from the Roman Wall to the sea, shadowing successively the wide landscapes of the marches. Historically, Elsdon was the capital of Redesdale at the centre of the Middle March and five tracks meet there. Its 17 acre (7ha) green was a dual-purpose area serving as a safe stockade for cattle when Scots swooped, a grazing-ground in more settled times, and a circular pound survives at its edge. St Cuthbert's Church and its graveyard divide a secluded upper green, with its fourteenth-century Vicar's Pele, the Rector's School, and a few cottages, from the larger, more open central and lower part, with pubs, cottages, and a few Georgian houses, almost all of grey stone, slate-roofed, and

111

modestly dignified. To paraphrase Orwell: if each English village is unique, Elsdon is more unique than most.

Cambo, however, on the Wallington estate to the south, is very much an estate village, although not all of one build or by one landowner. Sir Walter Blackett started its rebuilding in 1730, but not until 1911 did Sir George Trevelyan convert the old school-house (which Capability Brown attended from his home at nearby Kirkharle) into a village hall. A generation earlier, Sir Charles Trevelyan cleared many old buildings, making room for the neat terrace of South Row with its delightful front gardens. Beyond the Dolphin Fountain is the post office, housed in the medieval pele-tower, and wide views southwards over calm landscapes emphasise the serenity of Cambo and its caring owners.

The Coquet valley, particularly above Rothbury, is the loveliest in Northumberland. Lack of a road outlet beyond its remote head by the Roman camp at Chew Green on the Scottish border is no excuse for not exploring its lonely upper reaches. Harbottle and Alwinton are its last villages, tiny and quiet beneath rounded grassy hills threaded by ancient tracks from Scotland. Little remains of Harbottle's once proud castle, headquarters of the warden of the Middle March, and below its gaunt fragments is a single street of neat stone houses, a few unexpectedly large for so isolated a place, with gabled dormers and good masonry in their walls.

Warkworth, Northumberland. Grey sandstone houses line the street leading up to the castle

Warkworth, Northumberland. From the castle keep

At Alwinton, 2 miles (3.2km) up the valley, the Coquet escapes from its confined course to enter a landscape of hedged fields, giving the village a frontier character. The curlew symbol of the Northumberland National Park stands on the grass verge, and beyond are a few single-storey stone cottages, dispersed roughly in the form of an 'L' along one side of a green bisected by the Hosedon Burn. A farm, a pub – the Rose and Thistle – and the post office complete the community which comes to life in early October each year on the occasion of its Shepherds' Show.

By contrast, near the mouth of the Coquet, Warkworth enjoys the pride and kudos bestowed by six centuries of protection by one of the great northern castles of the Percys. Approached from the north, close to a rare fortified bridge, and up the hilly street with eighteenth-century houses, Warkworth's castle is seen to dominate the village. The entry from the south shows the wide colour range of its fine masonry, sandstones of grey, pink and buff, while the village houses are mainly grey, gaining their colour from pantile roofs. Handsome doorways, white woodwork, and classical proportions combine to produce a harmonious scene as good as any in England.

So, too, at Bamburgh farther north, where the castle is even more commanding, rock-perched above shining sands on one side and the village to

113

its west. Thus is Bamburgh a coastal village with no sea-front, with the heart of the village out of sight of the sea. Instead, nineteenth-century houses, many single-storey, all of grey stone, with roofs of slate or clay tile, face inwards to a small triangular green called The Grove, where trees shade a stone pump which makes a prominent focus. Some fringe development does not detract from the village quality which has an estate 'feel' about it, although this is not so apparent as that at Ford and Etal, in the Vale of Till, several miles inland. The first is essentially mid-nineteenth-century planned picturesqueness, a show-place of Victorian Northumberland, complete with a rebuilt fourteenth-century castle, all the work of the Countess of Waterford, with fine stonework, albeit in a Home Counties ethos. Etal is a little earlier, its single wide street tree-lined with whitewashed stone cottages, mainly roofed with heavy stone slates replacing the original thatch. A Georgian manor-house at one end of the village balances a small, ruined castle at the other.

A few miles north on the banks of the Tweed, Norham (pronounced Norrum) epitomises Northumberland. Ruins of its immense Norman castle look down the village street to St Cuthbert's Church. Bishop Pudsey, greatest builder in Durham's long line of prince-bishops, was responsible for starting both structures, and the castle was one of the headquarters of the bishops until 1844, when Norham and Holy Island ceased to be part of the Palatinate. The linear village, occupying low ground between the Tweed and the castle, focuses on a triangular green, where a medieval market cross stands on a seven-stepped plinth, its fish weather-vane a reminder of Norham's earlier dependence on Tweed salmon. Houses of warm, pink-brown sandstone, pantiled or slate-roofed, glow with colour, and apart from the bow-windowed Masons' Arms, are plain and unpretentious, illustrating northern reticence in a green setting.

Unique among English villages in being accessible by road only between the tides, Holy Island bestows a final benediction on the sandstone journey. There is no more romantic approach to an English village than this from the Northumbrian coast, by a causeway now extended along the sands to Holy Island village. This is an attractively colourful jumble of pink stone cottages, mainly single-storey with orange pantiles, although newer ones have slate roofs. Some earlier eighteenth-century houses seem to be built of hard, rough whinstone, white-mortared, the same type of rock as that on which Lindisfarne Castle is so majestically poised. Dobson's market cross on the square green is a neat focal point, but the glowing ruins of Lindisfarne Priory and the island's association with Saints Aidan and Cuthbert continue to make Holy Island a place of pilgrimage. Its secret is its special blend of saintly scholarship and serenity, of sand, sea and sky, and the haunting call of seabirds above the warm-tinted roofs of a friendly island village.

7

The Older Sandstones

Although it may not be the most attractive of our sandstones, gritstone is undoubtedly the strongest and most durable. Its geological name, Millstone Grit, emphasises its deep historical roots and evokes its uncompromising character. Gritstone is northern, tough and rugged, often containing large angular quartz grains, so that it has sometimes been mistaken for granite (as Charlotte Brontë did in *Jane Eyre*). Coarse and difficult to work, its impervious nature has encouraged its use since early times as a building stone, initially for castles, churches and bridges, and later for houses, farms and mills.

When freshly quarried, it varies in colour from dark grey to a pale sand, and it doesn't need sooty air to darken it, although atmospheric pollution accelerates the process of oxidation. So often it is seen grey-black beneath a grey Pennine sky, for gritstone is the main building stone of the southern Pennines where dark drystone walls run upwards from edges of towns and villages, binding them to the high, wild places on lonely moors of heather and tussocky grass. Farms and industrial villages hang below the moorland edge, secure and solid, yet always beyond them is the wilderness. Nearby, and on the hillsides, boundary walls of dark stone stitch bright green intake fields into a patterned embroidery, and in the valleys nineteenth-century mills give to the austere landscape a unique imprint of social history.

The River Trent roughly marks the gritstone's southern limit. Extending along both sides of the central plateau of Derbyshire's limestone uplands the gritstone follows on the east the great sweep of the Derwent valley and includes on the west the Staffordshire moorlands and a small slice of Cheshire. These two 'legs' of the gritstone pattern join near Edale to form a central trunk running northwards to the Aire Gap where the main area of stone broadens eastwards and then continues northwards to Richmond, across the Tees into west Durham and the northern Pennines, finally narrowing north-eastwards in Northumberland to meet the coast near Alnmouth. North of the Tyne, however, the gritstone is friable and easily eroded, resulting in low-lying landscapes far removed from the savage austerity of Pennine moors.

From Keighley the gritstone throws out an arm westwards into Lancashire to the Rossendale moors and Pendle country. North of the Ribble it creates the Bowland hills and extends from Morecambe Bay to the limestone landscapes near Settle on the edge of the Craven uplands.

Gritstone can be cut reasonably freely when quarry-fresh and was obtainable in large pieces, making it particularly suitable for window and door surrounds, lintels and mullions. Thus, over much of the Pennine gritstone country doors and windows have long stones forming jambs, lintels and sills; seventeenth- and eighteenth-century mullions are shaped, with later ones of simpler square section. Walls are almost invariably of large stones, regularly coursed, and, because stone darkens and mortar does not, joints are usually lighter coloured, an idiom emphasised in Lancashire by the practice of painting them white.

Houses of gritstone rarely show much decorative detail. Indeed, it would seem out of place. The only concession to fashion is likely to be the kneeler. Roofs themselves are usually of sandstone flags, large at the eaves, grading smaller to the ridge, heavy and necessarily low-pitched, rarely more than 30°, their weight ensuring stability.

Gritstone uplands have been sheep country since the Middle Ages, but by the early seventeenth century developments in the woollen industry brought conditions which allowed wealthy clothiers to build themselves new houses of stone. A gradual downward spread of wealth through society enabled people of other social groups to rebuild their own simple dwellings. An expansion of the domestic weaving industry during the late seventeenth and eighteenth centuries resulted in the construction of stone farmhouses and cottages with purpose-built workrooms for weaving, usually upstairs, but sometimes downstairs as well, lit by long rows of weavers' windows. These contain up to a dozen or more lights, separated by stone mullions, and many examples survive today especially in Pennine villages around Halifax, Huddersfield, Penistone, Oldham and Rochdale.

Even after machine spinning was introduced in small, water-powered mills, domestic weaving continued, and weavers' windows were still being built well into the nineteenth century. Gritstone continued to be used for the new terraces of mill-workers' cottages in most of the Pennine valleys and although many villages expanded rapidly into towns, they sometimes managed to preserve a semblance of village character at their heart.

To the north-east of Stoke-on-Trent beyond Cheadle and the wooded Churnet valley, the windswept, stone-walled landscape of the Staffordshire moorlands marks the beginning of the Peak District National Park. Brick gives way to dark stone, and the road which climbs beyond Froghall leads to gritstone uplands. Ipstones village, though sprouting much new building, shows its stonier character towards the western edge, away from the main road, and around St Leonard's church with its fine westward view. Further north and situated on a steep ridge between the Manifold and Dove valleys where the rivers are less than a mile (1.6km) apart, Longnor is one of the best of the

(opposite)
Longnor, Staffordshire. Dark gritstone, fine sandstone dressings and cobbled alleys

Staffordshire upland villages. In its broad cobbled market place the market hall still records the tolls exacted as recently as 1903. Chapel Street and Queen Street are narrow, stone-flagged passages leading between tall stone houses to the church's beckoning tower. Cobbles, flags, dark gritstone walls, sandstone quoins and lintels, and stone-slab roofs create a compact scene of solidity relieved by frequent glimpses southwards to the green pastures beyond the Manifold valley.

Still on the Staffordshire side of the Dove, with open views across the valley to Chrome Hill and Hollins Hill, a narrow winding road leads to the small, secluded hamlet of Hollinsclough, grouped around a cross-roads. The Bethel chapel of 1801 is a bit pompous and ostentatiously classical; down a lane is the later, but more restrained St Agnes Chapel with school adjoining. Village Farm and Vicarage Farm, both late classical, underline the rebuilding surge early last century which must have changed the appearance of this spot near the head of the Dove.

Flash lies just off the main Leek–Buxton road, north of the Roaches. Its pub, the New Inn, proudly displays on its sign 'Highest Village in England, 1518 feet above sea-level', justified if unenviable. The village still possesses a parish church and survives as a community in bleak, intimidating country. A short street of stone houses runs westwards from the church, behind the pub, and in this exposed situation it is not surprising to find stone-slab roofs weather-proofed with cement slurry, nor to read from its datestones that the church was built in 1744 and rebuilt 1901. Two centuries ago the village was large enough to merit a school, now the shop, with a plaque recording that it was founded in 1760. Flash must look forward to its short summer, when even the gritstone walls have verges and sward below yellowed with buttercups and bird's-foot trefoil, and fields are whitened with ox-eye daisies.

East of the White Peak, the A6 follows the narrowing Derwent valley northwards from Derby via Duffield, Matlock and Darley Dale. Milford has lost its historically interesting mill buildings, but above a bend in the river rows of gritstone cottages line the east side of the road with others behind on narrow terraces along the hillside, or clinging to the steep slopes of Hopping Hill.

Further up the Derwent, the dramatic situation and structure of Arkwright's mills, the self-assurance of an expanding industry, the innovation of 24-hour working and the good quality housing for the workers, all contributed to Cromford's becoming one of the earliest industrial stopping-off places on the British Tour, then entering its fashionable period. Cromford was Arkwright's village and is now a conservation area whose best street is undoubtedly North Street, leading off Cromford Hill. Built between 1771 and 1777 to house mill workers, it is vastly superior to most industrial housing, consisting of two rows of three-storeyed gritstone houses, darkly robust, with large slabs for lintels over windows and doors, and similar ones at the

Cromford, Derbyshire. North Street, built between 1771 and 1777. Three-storey mill-workers' houses in dark gritstone; flagged pavements

sides. The continuous lintel above the top storey suggests that the upper-floor windows may once have run the length of the street, illuminating a former long workshop, probably used for framework knitting. Regularly spaced stone mullions can still be identified. The school at the end of the street is a nineteenth-century addition. Houses on Cromford Hill are generally smaller, also of gritstone, and a few retain one single-light opening in their windows.

On the opposite side of the valley, Dethick, Lea and Holloway, usually referred to together and always in that order, sound more like a well-established firm of solicitors or estate agents than a trio of attractive stone villages. Hilltop farm buildings near Dethick church, Georgian façades at Lea, a riot of rhododendrons and azaleas in late spring, and fine views across the valley from Holloway, are rewards for exploring the narrow lanes above the Derwent. To the north-east, Ashover, only a few miles from Chesterfield and Clay Cross, manages to retain its gritty Peakland character, best revealed in the quiet area around the church.

Beyond Matlock's limestone surprises, Darley Dale is undistinguished, but to the west on Stanton Moor the gritstone is markedly lighter in colour than farther north in the heart of Peakland. Villages prefer to cling to the moor's western edge. Stanton-in-Peak really is the stone *tun* of its name, a village of attractive houses, mainly eighteenth century, clustered round small court-yards and alleyways tucked away off the main street which curves down the hill. WPT on a number of lintels signify the rebuilding in the 1830s by

William Paul Thornhill who also built the church. Birchover, at the southern end of the moor, enjoys an easier gradient, with houses set back from the road behind gardens.

The view from the northern edge of Stanton Moor reveals the calm and cultured contrast of the Chatsworth estates. Rowsley is a southern gateway both to these and to the Peak District National Park. Wye and Derwent meet in the village which is partly of nineteenth-century brick from its railway days, and warm-toned gritstone along its urban western arm where the Peacock Hotel looks as proud as its name, with many seventeenth- and eighteenth-century houses equally deserving our notice.

Beeley, Edensor and Pilsley are Chatsworth estate villages. Beeley retains a few seventeenth-century houses, Pilsley a few from Capability Brown's reorganisation of the park for the 4th Duke of Devonshire in the 1760s, and both have some of Paxton's early Victorian buildings. But Edensor best portrays the potential of the 'picturesque' much influenced by Blaise Hamlet, near Bristol, which Paxton had visited with the 6th Duke four years earlier in 1835. Paxton planned Edensor in the grandiose manner; Robertson of Derby designed most of its houses, deliberately fanciful in a variety of styles, Norman, Tudor, Swiss, castellated Gothic, each in its separate garden yet all grouped in an artificially steep-sided valley carefully hidden from view of Chatsworth House. In a parkland setting, the use of splendid stone throughout, with delightful details, a rich exuberance of chimneys compete for skyline attention with the focal point of the impressive spire of Scott's ducal church of 1869. Pilsley, a mile (1.6km) away, sits more comfortably into the green Derbyshire landscape, and broad greens lead to a single main street with neat unostentatious Paxton cottages of 1840, and, opposite the Devonshire Arms, a good group of a century earlier.

Baslow's nucleus is around the church at Bridge End where the narrow, humpy bridge no longer carries heavy vehicles but keeps its diminutive toll-house. Nether End developed round a green where the roads from Sheffield and Chesterfield converge near the Bar Brook. Squeezed on to the Derwent's east bank at the foot of gritstone moors, Baslow seems an afternoon type of place, catching the later sun which sparkles on the river, and touches up the textures of neat stone eighteenth-century houses. To the north, below the gritstone edges, Curbar, Froggatt and Nether Padley are scarcely keeping subtopian invasion at bay, within twenty minutes' drive of Chesterfield and Sheffield, splendidly situated, yet each retaining its core of older stone houses. Curbar seems the best, a piecemeal place, graced with productive gardens behind good stone walls. Even the old pinfold is now a garden, with the village well nearby, and along the bridlepath to Baslow the former eighteenth-century lock-up, now on private land, has one of Derbyshire's strangest roofs, conical and built up in layers of stone slabs.

Eyam, 2 miles (3.2km) beyond the Derwent, straddles a shelf 800ft (244m) up between the limestone of Middleton Dale and Eyam Moor to the north, an open, healthy situation which did not prevent its tragedy of 1665 when a box of clothing from London, sent to the village tailor, was contaminated with plague germs. Within days the disease spread; within weeks dozens had died, and within a year 250 of Eyam's 350 inhabitants had lost their lives. One of the Peak District's most attractive villages, more than most it has an indefinable villagey feel about it. Small, vaguely classical houses border an irregular square at its lower, eastern end, their thick gritstone walls and simple pitched roofs counterpointed by sliding sash-windows, small paned and homely. The main street curves gently uphill, a clump of trees blocking the view beyond. A mixture of houses lines the southern side, some with elegant Venetian windows, others in more simple vernacular style. Opposite is the nineteenth-century Gothic-style village school, and, set back from the road the church, with its famous pre-Conquest Eyam cross beside the path to the porch. More houses beyond, with institute and pub, and then, on the north side again the famous row of six seventeenth-century 'Plague Cottages', to one of which was delivered that fateful bale of cloth. Their simple gritstone structure shows to perfection the traditional style of Peakland domestic building.

Derbyshire is still a remarkably industrial county, and the road from Buxton which leads northwards to Chapel-en-le-Frith and Glossop illustrates this, with quarries, mills, viaducts, repeated reminders, and the Lancashire of L. S. Lowry never far away to the west. Chinley is still dominated by its magnificent curving viaduct; Hayfield a few miles north by the bulk of High Peak, and Kinder Scout itself.

Eyam

Hayfield is a large village, or small town, with a weekday workaday face and a weekend walkers' one. Packhorse routes converge, textiles are still made, and it is a fine starting point for Peakland explorers. Gritstone houses are cosily grouped, two or three storeyed, with woodwork white, while occasional datestones indicate eighteenth-century building activity.

There is no road running northwards along the Pennines. The dark, powerful beauty of High Peak and the South Pennine moors is for walkers; theirs is the empty, spacious landscape, seen and sometimes sensed by travellers on the trans-Pennine roads linking Yorkshire with Greater Manchester and Lancashire.

A mere cock-stride from Oldham, their names tolling an euphonic greeting, are Dobcross, Denshaw, Diggle and Delph, all formerly in a long West Riding finger, but now generically in the Saddleworth district of Greater Manchester. Until the turnpike and canal were almost simultaneously established around 1800, Dobcross was the main village in the area, and still has a concentrated wealth of weavers' houses of that date, closely grouped around the tiniest of squares. A fifteen-light upper window characterises one row of three-storey houses, while at nearby Delph, a larger village, the post office has a twelve-light example overlooking the main street. Behind the houses are small mill buildings of the late eighteenth and early nineteenth centuries. At Tame, between Delph and Denshaw, there is a farmhouse known to have existed in 1642 with additions made at various times both front and back, and an extra floor added in 1780 to house handlooms, with the usual set of mullioned windows.

Similar examples of organic growth of existing buildings can be seen by exploring the environs of Saddleworth. High Kinders, at Greenfield, has a 1642 datestone, and it is apparent what extensions were made, probably about 1780, when the woollen industry flourished and the place was a focus of domestic weaving. Saddleworth Fold, Butterhouse, Bunkers and Shepherd's Fold provide similarly powerful visual evidence of structural changes between the seventeenth and late eighteenth centuries, so that a visit to Saddleworth is as rewarding for the industrial archaeologist as it is for the stone village 'buff'.

When strong westerlies bring rain clouds scudding over the bare, treeless slopes, huddles of houses, dark Victorian churches and darker mills, and sunlight breaks through to glisten on shiny rooftops or gleam on bright green fields, throwing up in harsh relief the wandering walls, then are these northern industrial landscapes touched with magic. Nowhere else in Britain has quite the same pattern, nowhere the same proportions of shapes and tones and textures, nowhere quite the same brooding beauty.

Travel north-east by the A62 to Marsden and the Colne Valley, or by the A635 over Wessenden Moor to Holmfirth and the Holme valley, and you soon realise the very definite nature of these valleys, clefts in the hills, with weaving communities built along the sides, sometimes terraced, sometimes excitingly

Dobcross, Greater Manchester. Gritstone, with light-coloured mortar. Weavers' houses from the late eighteenth century, showing loom-shop windows on the upper floor

climbing the steep slopes. The northernmost part of the Peak District National Park reaches to within 5 miles (8km) of the centre of Huddersfield, and Marsden, Slaithwaite, Meltham and Holmfirth are just outside it, yet each village, or small town, keeps a sturdy independence.

As with the villages on the western side, there is a high-level zone of cottages almost on the moor edge, stone-built and therefore giving the appearance of prosperity. Many weavers' windows have been replaced, unfortunately, by large 'picture' windows. Groups of cottages subsequently formed folds and hamlets, and later, terraces of textile-workers' cottages were added to the hillsides, or built close to the valley mills, creating compact villages. Most settlements in the Pennine valleys around Huddersfield and Halifax show this dual character.

Golcar, on the outskirts of Huddersfield, is never likely to feature in the 'prettiest village' competition. Its terraces face south across the steep Colne valley to catch the sunlight which fails to lighten their tones. Narrow roads slide down between high gables and there is not much greenery. Dozens of weavers' cottages with typical large windows in the top floors light the weaving-room which was also the bedroom until about 1800. From then until around the middle of last century, new three-storey houses had the top-floor loom-shops completely cut off from the rest of the house, and usually given a separate rear entrance by an outside stair. Many Golcar houses have well-cut stone mullions and neatly ashlared lintels and door surrounds. Stone-flagged paths in front, flagged floors inside, and stone-slab roofs above all create an uncompromising solidity as attractive in its own way as mellowed Cotswold oolite with which, in one respect, it shared an economic parentage – wool. A group of three weavers' cottages now houses the Colne Valley Museum which re-creates the domestic and working conditions experienced by spinners and weavers around 1800. Nearby, new houses tucked into levelled areas of hillside are of honey-coloured gritstone, in designs sympathetic to the traditional local idiom, and by no means look out of place.

Across the valley, Clough and Linthwaite follow a similar pattern, though more muted, while over the hill Meltham is closer to the moors yet more urban. Honley and Almondbury have spawned new housing estates, and north of Huddersfield villages have grown, merged and, for the most part, have lost their identities. However, north of the trans-Pennine motorway, Ripponden is a splendid survival, the only village in the valley of the Ryburn which quickly runs northwards to join the Calder at Sowerby Bridge. The old heart of the village, grouped loosely round the church, is a conservation area, much more intimate than Colne valley villages.

One of the valley-bottom main roads, the A646, follows the River Calder, probably the most rewarding of all Pennine valleys in which to see the landscape changes of the past seven centuries which led to the eventual marriage of farming and weaving, their subsequent divorce, and the unrivalled legacy of seventeenth- and eighteenth-century houses built of local gritstone at the peak of the dual-economy system, and the grimmer nineteenth-century terraces which followed.

Until about 1250 most settlements were near the moor edge, but shortage of suitable land and population growth necessitated a gradual movement towards the valley where new farms were created. By the late fifteenth century it had become necessary for people to supplement the meagre rewards resulting from farming in a hostile environment, so they turned to woollen manufacture. By the late seventeenth century a dual-economy was flourishing, continuing until the 1850s, when power looms were in general use in the large mills which had sprung up in the mushrooming towns. When this happened, hill villages went into decline, the reasons for their existence having gone.

Heptonstall, West Yorkshire. Hilltop village of domestic weavers. Most houses are eighteenth-
and early nineteenth-century

Their village character survived, and today they are unique, remarkably
unaltered, almost native in character, and full of surprises.

Heptonstall is best, a hill-crest village of attractive houses, mainly
two-storey but with a few larger ones, darkly handsome, austere. Its single
main street climbs steadily to 900ft (274m), with folds and short terraces
leading from it. Saunter it to savour it, and enjoy the symphonic splendour of
its stone buildings. At the core is its ruined medieval church surrounded by a
graveyard whose massive memorials now lie as horizontal flags all around,
shadowed by the massive bulk of a proud Victorian successor. Nearby is the old
Cloth Hall of about 1550, converted into cottages about 1700 and given a
second storey fifty years later. The grammar school below the churchyard,
endowed in 1642, now houses a local history museum, and Weavers' Square,
north of the church, on a site previously occupied by cottages, is itself a little
museum of stone, using most types of Yorkshire paving, including gritstone

125

and granite setts, sandstone flags, and cobbles and pebbles from the River Calder. Correctly, if perversely, it naturally includes concrete. Nearby, a street sign depicts 'Top oth Town', and a couple of hundred yards away, near the village's northern edge, the octagonal Methodist chapel of 1764 claims to be the oldest in continual use.

Heptonstall, true to the stone itself, is clean-edged. To its south and east are steep valley sides, with mills and chimneys far below at Hebden Bridge. To the west is an instant transition to stone-walled fields and then the wide, windswept village of Slack, and the historic, lonely road across the Pennines to Burnley, the Long Causeway. Away to the south, across the Calder valley, Stoodley Pike points its monumental finger to the sky, beyond another remarkable survivor, Mankinholes. In this tiny village almost every building is a fine seventeenth-century house, and by the roadside is an unusual group of drinking troughs for watering the many packhorse trains which came this way during the seventeenth and eighteenth centuries, using the miles of stone-flagged moorland causeways across the moors.

To complete a trio of stone villages from the riches of Calderdale, Luddenden must be included. Crammed into the mouth of a narrow valley, with cobbled streets and gritstone houses sometimes four storeys high, it demands exploring on foot. Its valley is generous with trees and birds, lively with swiftly running waters. Its memories are of cottage industry, and – in the seventeenth-century Lord Nelson inn in the square below the church – of Branwell Brontë during his two years as booking-clerk at Luddenden Foot station. Above the square the village school has, by way of a ground-floor or basement, a pair of adjoining lock-ups labelled Midgley and Warley, since the parish boundary between the two once passed through the middle of the

Slack

Haworth, West Yorkshire. Main Street: cobbles, weavers' houses, and hills in every view

building. Beyond the village, the green hillsides of Luddenden Dean typify the contrasts which characterise the Calderdale landscape.

Were it not for the Brontë family, Haworth would be as native a village as Heptonstall or Golcar. Expansion of the textile trade in the late eighteenth century gave it a legacy of huddled houses and untidy streets, all of which appalled Maria Brontë when her parson husband Patrick brought her and the young children there in 1820. What the Brontë pilgrims see today is a romanticised ideal. Once the sprawling housing estates and straggle of mills are penetrated, Haworth's core is still the steep uneven street, kept cobbled in deference to the past, which toils up to the Bull, the church and the parsonage. Most of the weavers' windows of the dark stone houses have gone, but the atmosphere of melancholy remains, nowhere so much as in the churchyard crammed with graves. Experienced on a dank November day, the year's dying fall distils the Brontë essence, the starkness, the tragedy, the genius and the ghosts. It is not difficult to feel that at any moment Heathcliff himself might come striding from the moors beyond the village.

Lonely moor roads from Heptonstall and Haworth cross the Pennine watershed into north-east Lancashire where, beyond Burnley, Nelson and Colne, and always away from main roads, splendid stone villages are the rule rather than the exception. Wycoller, in a secretive valley near Trawden, above Colne, is a tiny hamlet revitalised through sensible conservation, with everything of grey-brown stone. A ruined hall ('Ferndean Manor' of *Jane Eyre*),

Downham, Lancashire. Warm brown sandstone, with Pendle Hill beyond

Waddington, Lancashire. Sandstone, some rendered and colour-washed. Cobbles and stone-slate roofs

a sparkling beck spanned by ancient bridges, close-grouped houses and cottages, generous trees and memories of weaving days are uniquely distilled in one of the North's unique places.

To the west, Pendle Hill has its own memories, of witchcraft in early Stuart times. Villages which ring it show stone houses set against its brooding presence. Sabden, Higham, Newchurch and Barley on its southern and eastern flanks all suffer from having too much painted masonry, but in each there is at least one notable house or group that proclaims its true character. A terrace near Sabden church shows stone-mullioned, two-light windows, stone-slate roofs and gay front gardens. Houses of early Victorian days are higher, front directly on to pavements, and have long roof lines of dark slate which follow the slope of a street. Higham's main street is distinguished by a pair of splendid porched barns facing each other, with one fine house nearby retaining a multi-light weavers' window in its upper floor.

Downham, at Pendle's northern foot, is a gem by any standards, mainly the result of the influence of many generations of the Assheton family. Early last century two Asshetons, father and son, gave the village most of the appearance it enjoys today, building the vicarage and school, refronting the hall and improving the church. Downham straggles up a hill with southward views to Pendle, with seventeenth-century houses by a brook and bridge at the bottom,

handloom weavers' houses around the green, and the hall beyond the church. Each detail satisfies, the whole delights.

South of Clitheroe, Whalley has expanded but keeps a village character. Extensive remains of its large Cistercian abbey survive, especially the great gateway, but after the Dissolution of the Monasteries, much of its dressed masonry subsequently found its way into the walls of local farms and houses, although little seems to be visible in Whalley's cottages, the best of which are in a terrace north of the church. Across the Ribble, Waddington benefits by having a brook running down its length, with gardens to the houses flanking each side, and flowers in profusion. Trees and grass are a perfect foil to unpretentious cottages, mainly showing their dark stone, with pronounced quoins, but a few rendered and colour-washed, with dark-painted window surrounds. Occasional small squares create satisfying open spaces, and the stone ethos is enhanced here and there by cobbles.

Further down the Ribble, many of Ribchester's houses reflect its pre-industrial prosperity between 1790 and 1825 when it was an important centre of handloom weaving, the cotton yarn coming from Preston and Blackburn. Weavers worked in their homes, so that large rooms were needed as loom-shops as well as for storing raw materials and finished cloth. Cottages in Church Street are good examples, Nos 61–2 showing very well the large masonry blocks used in front walls, even bigger lintels and sills, stone-mullioned basement loom-shop windows, and raised front doors with a typical date-panel above. The ostentatious doorway of No 56, one of a row built three years previously, obviously copies the style of a grander house. Near the village centre the White Bull, dated 1707, has a porch canopy on four Tuscan columns thought to be from the Roman fort of AD80, most of whose ruins lie beneath the streets of the village.

Beyond Longridge Fell to the north, Chipping was, until the seventeenth century, the village whose market served a wide area of pastoral and hill country around the Hodder valley. More than any other Lancashire village does it have a near-Cotswold character, although its stone is darker, rougher, more northern. Many of its houses date from the seventeenth century when the local wool trade peaked and flax-spinning had also become important. A curving street of cottages flanks the churchyard, with Windy Street leading southwards past John Brabin's village school and nearby almshouses of 1684, the former with a richly decorated porch, the latter merely having simple slate canopies. Cobbled pavements and courtyards are tucked away; stone-mullioned windows and slate-stone roofs, together with the rubble-stone walls

---

(*opposite*)

Ribchester, Lancashire. Church Street: loom-workers' houses with basement loom-shop. Large blocks of gritstone and a slate date-panel

Chipping, Lancashire. Delight in detail: worked masonry and neat cobbles of Chipping's houses harmonise to produce a picture of a near perfect village, marred only by occasional over-restoration and prettification.

To the north, Slaidburn shelters in a fold below the heathery moors of Bowland Forest, where the Croasdale Brook joins the upper reaches of the River Hodder. Short rows of stone cottages toe cobbled pavements in the main street, their masonry showing the 'waterthrow' tilt, with lines of mortar picked out by sunlight, and footings standing proud. Large blocks of neatly dressed sandstone boldly frame windows and doorways fronted by scrubbed flagstones. The whole village is a delight in stone, highlighted by the Hark to Bounty inn with its exterior staircase, and the elegant grammar school whose carved plaque proclaims its foundation by John Brennand in 1717.

Below Bowland's northern edge the villages along the Lune valley complement a serenely pastoral landscape backed by hills. The A683 Lancaster–Kirkby Lonsdale road links them, with Hornby the most prominent, a single broad street of good stone houses and inns, and a church with an octagonal tower, with Hornby Castle in its riverside parkland dominating the view from the bridge. Melling, 2 miles (3.2km) north, smaller and more compact, has a higher proportion of fine seventeenth-century road-hugging houses, their thick walls rose-garlanded, with mullioned windows and long roofs of grey stone-slates. In another 2 miles (3.2km), across the Greta, Tunstall provides a convenient literary link to take us back to the Yorkshire gritstone which we had left at Haworth. When the Brontë sisters were at Lowood School they walked on Sundays to matins at Tunstall church, situated in pastures outside the village, ate packed lunches in the chamber above the porch and returned to Cowan Bridge after evensong.

Keighley is near the northern end of Pennine gritstone country. From there a narrow band of the rock runs westwards to Blackburn and Chorley, and a widening belt extends eastwards to the edge of Leeds, then northwards almost to the Tees. Between the Carboniferous Limestone of the Yorkshire Dales and the narrow strip of dolomite (see Chapter 2) along the edge of the Vale of York, gritstone villages abound, industrialised in Airedale and lower Nidderdale, rural to the north.

Middlesmoor, almost 1,000ft (305m) up at the head of Nidderdale, has probably the most dramatic view of any northern village, embracing all of this sylvan valley, jewelled with Gouthwaite Reservoir. Dark stone houses are close-clustered, scarcely two on the same level, and rising direct from the winding streets, and with cobbled paths between. Headstones in the

Ripley, North Yorkshire. Mid-nineteenth-century village: Victorian Gothic housing in fine dark sandstone. Market cross and stocks on cobbles make an important focus in an open area

churchyard appear to tumble down the slope as though determined to fall into the neat, tidy Ramsgill, ordered around its green far below.

Near the lower end of Nidderdale, Ripley shows the calm harmony of a planned village, which it is. I much prefer its immaculate gentility, with an occasional bravura introduction, to the overpowering fortes of Edensor. The Ingilbys have been at Ripley for over six centuries, in the Tudor castle greatly altered in 1780. In 1827–8 Sir William Amcott Ingilby replaced the old thatched cottages of the village with sturdy, gritstone two-storey houses along both sides of the road running at right-angles to the cobbled square. Behind broad grass verges, and framed by trees, the houses are generously Tudor-Gothic, with detailed dressings above windows and doors, and deep eaves. A flamboyant *pièce de résistance* is the 'Hotel de Ville', as it is prominently inscribed, with proud battlements and huge mullioned windows, dating from 1854 and completed by his widow after Sir William's death. It is now the

(opposite)

Plate 6 (above) Muker, North Yorkshire. Pennine austerity in grey-brown sandstone of upper Swaledale. Most of the housing was for local lead-miners of the late eighteenth and early nineteenth centuries; *(below)* Blisland, Cornwall. Newly restored Mansion House on the edge of a rare Cornish village green. Grey-brown granite in walls, quoins, lintels, fancy finials, topped by a fine slate roof

village hall and post office. Old market cross, village stocks, and fourteenth-century parish church with visible reminders of Civil War days, and a rare 'weeping cross', complete a picture of one of the most attractive of the northern villages.

Harewood, between Leeds and Harrogate, is far grander, built by John Carr of York in 1760 along the approach to the main gates of Harewood House. One terrace of two-storey cottages in vernacular style was designed as a ribbon factory, to provide local employment, while other blocks are given an almost urban elegance by adding a half or whole storey, with sophisticated arches above upper windows and giant blank arches linking groups. An impressive inn was built by the main Leeds road but the church was left undisturbed close to the 'big house'. Early nineteenth-century landscaping added front gardens to the houses, many of which were also lowered in height without diminishing their assured elegance. All the stone was quarried locally.

In the northern dales of Yorkshire very fine-grained gritstones occur, usually in the top strata of the Yoredale Series, and capable of being cut cleanly into good building stones. Layers of well-bedded sandstones are also found within the Yoredales, with the result that throughout Wensleydale and Swaledale villages possess a distinctive unity – but not uniformity – which matches some of the most beautiful and harmonious landscapes in Britain. Soft green turf, grey-white limestone scars etching hillsides, with stone walls stitching the steep slopes and patterning the valleys ensure that this area could be nowhere else in England, colourful but soft and muted in greys and greens and shades of brown, into which the villages nestle comfortably on the well-drained gravels on the edges of the valley floor.

Jervaulx Abbey gives its benediction to the eastern approach up Wensleydale. To the west in East Witton, small unpretentious stone houses, detached or in pairs, border opposite sides of an elongated green, in the planned perfection expected from a total rebuilding of 1819 when the Earl of Ailesbury took over the Jervaulx Abbey estate. An old estate map proves that the present houses and gardens occupy the same positions as they had done in 1627, and a similar layout existed at the Dissolution of the Monasteries a century earlier.

Nearby, Middleham's massive twelfth-century castle broods over the large, compact village whose two market squares and three-storey houses and inns give it an urban appearance and character. History and present-day inhabitants would accord it town status, and its imporance as a race-horse training centre spans more than two centuries. Far longer, however, are its memories of Richard Neville, Earl of Warwick, and his more famous son-in-law, Richard, Duke of Gloucester, who married Anne Neville in 1474, the couple making their home at the castle until Richard's coronation as Richard III in 1483.

All of Wensleydale's villages are good, many are memorable. West Burton and Bainbridge have generous, well-kept greens, Carperby and Castle Bolton

Askrigg, North Yorkshire. Delight in detail: date-panel in carved gritstone lintel and a house wall of brown sandstone

Askrigg

align themselves along the road, and Askrigg's three-storey houses bordering the street which curves down a hill to a small cobbled market place indicate an eighteenth-century importance. Many lintels and window dressings are of Millstone Grit, carefully hauled from the fell-top 2 miles (3.2km) away, and almost 1,000ft (305m) above the village. Sandstone flags, graded in size from eaves to ridge, are the universal roofing material, and roof pitches of rarely more than 30° echo the profile of distant hillsides.

Individual buildings are rarely outstanding, although most villages do have one or two fine seventeenth-century houses, some with projecting, two-storeyed gabled porches, as at Bainbridge, Countersett and Thoralby. But it is the whole in its setting which distinguishes most villages in the Yorkshire Dales, none more so than Bainbridge whose road approaches at opposite ends of the rectangular green are such as to ensure closed views of the inward-facing houses, and beyond them the familiar green hills of Wensleydale.

Swaledale is steeper sided and more sinuous than Wensleydale, tinged with melancholy of vanished industry. Lead-mining flourished in the dale during

Thwaite
Swaledale.

the eighteenth and nineteenth centuries, and villages were enlarged then. Almost all are on the south-facing side of the dale – Healaugh, Low Row, Gunnerside, Muker and Thwaite. Gunnerside, at the foot of its ravine-like tributary gill, and Muker, at the foot of Kisdon, are memorable in setting and appearance, compact, clustered, clean, always within sound of laughing waters, and sheltered by friendly hills. Look across to Gunnerside from the Crackpot road south of the river, between a framework of silver birches; admire Muker, or Thwaite, from the Pennine Way track on Kisdon, or, less energetically from the road to Keld, and you'll see the perfect dales landscape of valley, hill, village, stone walls and field barns. Man's contributions are wholly harmonious; even the quarries from which came the splendid sandstone are hidden away in quiet folds of the hills, and most of the lead-mining scars are in remote valleys.

Keld is the last village in the dale, a tiny place dwarfed by lonely fells, in a hollow by a limestone gorge, and from it narrow roads wind steadily upwards, one crossing the Pennine watershed beyond the source of the Swale to Kirkby

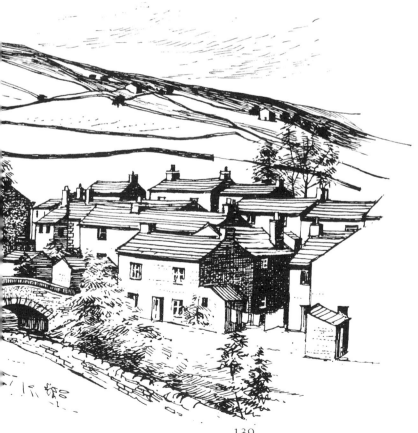

Stephen, another heading north to Tan Hill inn, branching there to Appleby, or turning eastwards down Arkengarthdale, past more lead-mining hamlets, to Reeth and Swaledale again. Reeth's large sloping green, backed by elegant three-storey inns and hotels, looks eastwards down the broad valley. A mecca for weekend visitors, and another example of a large dales village where there is hardly an individual building of great merit, but the unplanned grouping, the unity of local materials which imparts so great a visual appeal, is the secret of its character and attraction.

Upper Teesdale differs from all other Pennine valleys. Middleton-in-Teesdale is the main settlement, a small, friendly town developed last century as the centre of an important lead-mining area, but beyond that is David Bellamy's 'Upper Dale' of his pioneering book *The Great Seasons*, where clouds pile up over spacious uplands, and farms and hamlets on the Raby estates are all whitewashed. Below Middleton, however, Teesdale is generously wooded, almost sylvan, and in such a setting Romaldkirk is one of the most perfect of northern villages. Stone houses border in delightful informality a number of greens and the intimate view in any direction is one of remarkable balance with occasional accents on a larger Georgian house, an inn or two, and the village stocks. Stone walls, gardens, mature trees, and a stately church contribute to the overall sense of harmony, while lanes and footpaths lead from the greens in all directions, to Middleton, to Eggleston, to Cotherstone, to the river, and to the moors.

Romaldkirk is only one of many villages in Durham which have greens. Indeed, the broad, usually rectangular green is a noticeable characteristic of this under-appreciated county, more commonly orientated with its longer axis east-west and a road running along its length. Normally, no buildings encroach on its grass other than, perhaps, the church, well, smithy and Victorian school. Farms, houses and cottages front the green in a layout which in many cases has survived from Anglo-Saxon times. Staindrop, a few miles north-east of Barnard Castle, is one of Durham's most attractive green-villages, one which became prominent in medieval days under the powerful influence of the Nevilles who had lived at nearby Raby since 1061. In 1378, when the Bishop of Durham gave Lord John Neville licence to crenellate his castle, Staindrop acquired its market charter. The village, with mainly eighteenth-century houses of sandstone, many of them whitewashed, some having three storeys, extends for more than ½ mile (0.8km) along a series of interlocking greens which narrow towards the eastern end, thus focusing attention on a distinguished parish church.

To the north is Cockfield, 750ft (229m) up on the southern edge of open commonland pockmarked by a remarkable number of earthworks, ranging from Romano-British enclosures to abandoned quarries and waggonways of last century. The village has a two-row plan, with long tofts to the north, and mainly nineteenth-century houses of yellow-brown stone obtained locally.

Cockfield's industrial background provides a fascinating contrast to that of Staindrop, and its clean, open sturdy appearance is far removed from that of Durham's mining villages to the east.

To the north and west the Pennine landscapes of west Durham become wilder and more austere, subject to road-blocking snowfalls in winter. Sombre dark moors replace Teesdale's spacious green fells, and valleys reveal more evidence of vanished industry. Small cottages of brown sandstone, built for and by lead-miners and quarrymen last century, characterise the villages of Weardale and the twin Allendales over the watershed to the north. Wolsingham developed as a small market town serving the lower dale, and retains a good range of stone buildings appropriate to seventeenth- and eighteenth-century importance, and industrial growth last century through local ironworks. Walls are of dressed stone or rubble, with roofs of stone slabs or slates. Meadhope Street shows typical dales' architecture, but Whitfield Cottages in the market place, dated 1677, recently restored, are outstanding.

Stanhope fulfils the function of a small town for the mid-dale area, while higher up Weardale villages are compactly linear in plan, often sprouting short terraces along hillsides, as at Westgate, Daddry Shield and Ireshopeburn. St John's Chapel has the only Anglican church in the upper dale, an austere building of 1752 which for size, if not beauty, gains pride of place in a village of sandstone terraces. The road out of the valley head passes new afforestation on hillsides formerly scarred by old lead-mine workings and leads over the watershed at Killhope Cross, at 2,056ft (627m) the highest point on any A-class road in England. Just across the Cumbrian border is Nenthead, enjoying life at 1,400ft (427m), a village whose present appearance is mainly the result of enterprising plans of the Quaker London Lead Company between 1800 and 1850 to rehouse workers and their families, as well as providing social and educational facilities. Local sandstone was used throughout, and although the village could in no way be described as pretty, it is perhaps a minor-key north Pennine equivalent to the much more famous Cromford in Derbyshire.

Minor roads climb northwards from Weardale to the Allendales, parallel northward-facing valleys, beautiful yet melancholy with memories of eighteenth- and nineteenth-century lead-mining under the Beaumont and Blackett family influences. Allendale Town became the centre of lead-mining in Northumberland and also lays claim to be at the geographical centre of Britain. Rows of warm-toned sandstone houses of sturdy simplicity radiate from a wide square, softened by trees, but tourism has replaced lead-mining as the chief local trade. Planted woodlands on the hillsides enclosing Allenheads give necessary protection to a remote settlement established around lead-mines, dressing floors and workshops.

Across the watershed to the east, 2 miles (3.2km) above the Derwent Reservoir, and near the head of the River Derwent, is one of the great surprises

of these northern Pennines. Blanchland is both a paradox and a little paradise. Trees clothe the lower moorland slopes which shelter the village in its valley setting. Trim, buff-coloured cottages in neat rows line the sides of a large 'L'-shaped square (if you can have such a shape!) in courtyard fashion. And that is its secret, for Blanchland today is the result of a complete restoration of an older village carried out by the trustees of the Lord Crewe estate (he was formerly one of the Durham prince-bishops) from 1752 onwards. They retained the original collegiate layout of the village, which, five years earlier, according to John Wesley, was 'little more than a heap of ruins'. It must have been so for almost two centuries after the dissolution of its abbey in 1539 and after suffering from Scottish raids.

Blanchland Abbey was founded in 1165 by a Premonstratensian order of monks (whose white habit gave rise to the name), and parts of the thirteenth-century abbey church survive as the parish church, and part of the abbey refectory and guest-house are incorporated into the eighteenth-century Lord Crewe Arms. The former gatehouse is a central focus in the village square, and now contains a shop; the stone cottages were built to house lead-miners who worked in the various local mines established in the mid-eighteenth century, making this moorland village one of the earliest and best of industrial settlements.

Beyond the Tyne the Northumbrian uplands roll away northwards in a series of ridges to the Simonside Hills above Rothbury and the Cheviots beyond the Coquet. Cloud shadows drift eastwards across a lonely landscape of distant horizons, and in this vast empty region farm-hamlets are the rule, villages the exception, a pattern associated with the uneasy centuries of Border strife which resulted in so much of Northumberland not being developed for farming until well into the eighteenth century.

(*opposite*)

Blanchland, Northumberland. Mid-eighteenth-century planned village on a monastic foundation. Dark stone houses around a large central square. Flagstones, cobbles and a medieval gatehouse concentrate the interest

8
The Hardest Rocks

On the Geological Survey Ten Mile Map only half a dozen areas in England are coloured bright red. These are the regions of the hard rock, granite and its associates, and, apart from the Lake District and a minute blob in Leicestershire, the far south-west has the greatest number, with Cornwall claiming the lion's share. However, much of that county is on the Old Red Sandstone, an easier material to handle, so the number of granite villages is limited. In Devon, too, granite has had a restricted use, so that only on the edges of Dartmoor are you likely to find villages where granite, rather than cob, slate or sandstone, predominates.

Granites vary, but all contain three essential minerals, quartz, felspar and mica. The first two are extremely hard and almost indestructible, while mica, though soft and easily scratched, is impervious to water and chemical weathering. Thus, granite's greatest characteristics are strength and durability. No natural building material is tougher, which makes it ideal where impregnability is the first consideration. But this is not a quality necessarily sought in cottages and small houses. Equally, its hardness allows for little refinement or decoration, nor does its colour show much variety, limited as it is by the range of tints of the felspar crystals, usually red, pink, grey or white, sometimes very pale green, and occasionally combining to give a mottled appearance.

Against these apparent disadvantages can be offset the splendid textural quality of granite in its unpolished state and its complete lack of stratification. These virtues are better appreciated in the small scale rather than the large, so that mouldings at doorways and windows look more attractive than large areas of granite, which present a monotonous appearance. Its hardness makes granite expensive to work into blocks of similar size with the result that granite masonry is rarely coursed, but shows a rugged, often crude, but timeless face to the world. Generally speaking, the older buildings contain the biggest blocks of stone, as is revealed in a glance at stones used in the bases of many Cornish church towers.

Compared to limestones, granite shows two other negative qualities. It is a poor reflector of light, so even on the brightest days there is no glow to a granite house, although cold winter sunlight gives it a silvery appearance. At the same time, because there is only the shallowest cutting between adjacent blocks, and there is little or no moulded detail, few shadows are cast. Since the effect of alternating light and shadow contributes so much life to a single wall, a village of granite buildings is visually remarkably uniform and grey. Presumably, this is one reason why granite cottages so frequently have their base stone obscured beneath colour-wash, usually white or pink. It can hardly be used for protection.

Cornish granite, commonly a pale silvery-grey colour, occurs in four main areas from Land's End to Bodmin Moor, and it is in these areas where granite villages may be found. The Penwith peninsula is the most westerly of them, where Cornwall narrows towards its tip, and all the hard, stony character of the county, which makes it so distinctive from the rest of England, seems to concentrate its essence. Cornwall is a land of stone, and almost everything is made of stone, picked initially as moorstone from the surface of the windswept moors. Prehistoric man used it for his burial places; Bronze Age and Iron Age dwellers, clearing boulders from the wastes, created the first field boundaries, and even took the granite underground to line the walls of their fogous. As late as the fifteenth century moorstone was used, rough hewn on the spot, and taken to build those austere Cornish churches which have such a unique appearance and endearing quality. Sentinel on lonely uplands or sheltered in deep, hidden combes, they are the characteristic village marks of Cornwall. In villages themselves a feature surviving from pre-Reformation days is the holy well, often with a neat granite structure raised above it in the sixteenth

Chysauster

century. Few village houses are as old as this, however, most of them being of eighteenth- and nineteenth-century dates, those in the tin-mining and granite-quarrying areas rarely more than 150 years old.

Cornwall has the oldest stone village in England. North of Penzance, Penwith's elemental landscape is all space and sky, rock and sea, where granite outcrops crest the hills, granite walls divide the fields, and granite cliffs stand bulwark to the waves. Lonely on gorsey uplands, Chysauster has been deserted now for seventeen centuries, but for almost four hundred years before then it was a village of our Celtic ancestors. Excavations have revealed details of five of its nine courtyard houses, their lower walls of roughly coursed, unmortared granite almost 6ft (1.8m) high, flanking what was the village street. Each house has a passage leading to an open courtyard with tiny rooms leading off, and terraced gardens behind. Covered drains, open hearths, and stone basins where grain was ground are not dissimilar to those used by Romans, whose early period of settlement in Britain overlapped the second half of Chysauster's occupation.

Penwith's bony uplands seem almost as bare and bleak as the distant Hebrides. Small, irregular, granite-bounded fields fringe the windy road that sweeps along the northern coast of Cornwall's toe from St Ives to Land's End. There is music in the names Zennor, Morvah, Pendeen, Botallack and St Just, and melancholy in the gaunt grey ruins of hollow engine-houses, roofless granite towers with narrowing brick chimneys, memorials of tin-mining days.

Zennor, Cornwall. Granite boulders by the approach to a granite village in the Penwith peninsula

Zennor, sheltering in a hollow behind Zennor Head, reached by a switchback road with massive granite boulders always in the view, is a cluster of granite farms in a treeless landscape of small fields bounded by stone walls. Only the yellow gorse in spring paints in splashes of colour, vivid against the blue Atlantic. Whitewash lifts the greyness; church and pub (The Tinners' Arms) are essential nuclei, and the Wayside Museum, housed in an old mill, reveals with pride various exhibits of the domestic, rural and industrial past.

The tin-mining ethos pervades St Just, almost a town, with terraces of nineteenth-century cottages, colour-washed and trim. Brilliant Cornish light produces hard shadows, emphasising contrasts to the point of harshness. Was there such colour a century ago? I doubt it. Three streets converge on Plan-an-Guare (The Plane), a large, clock-towered square near the church. Front gardens soften the austerity; some houses sport porches with coloured glass, but nothing can disguise the prim geometry of plain, Victorian windows, usually one-up, one-down, so often characteristic of miners' terraces throughout the country.

The roads around St Just are graced with Cornwall's most decorative and well-kept milestones, single blocks of granite, usually white-painted, with good lettering of place-names and distances, and pointing hands. But villages tend to consist of a row or two of neat stone cottages, usually colour-washed, along the road, by a grey-towered church, proud chapel, or lonely by a former mine or quarry.

Across the peninsula Mousehole is a large village on Mount's Bay. Houses of slate and grey-brown granite, some colourwashed, others rendered, rise untidily in narrow streets and alleys from the east-facing sheltered harbour where fishing still predominates over tourism.

At Godolphin Cross, dark stone cottages grouped at a cross-roads has more of a feudal feel about it, which is hardly surprising in view of a long association with the Godolphin family who rose to eminence in Tudor times. Godolphin Hall itself gained ephemeral fame through its use for the 'Poldark' series.

On the Lizard peninsula, Serpentine, an igneous rock like granite, usually dark green or grey but occasionally brownish, and often mottled in a mixture of shades, has been quarried for building stone. Some of Cadgwith's thatched cottages are made of it, but most are granite, white-washed as is common in fishing villages. Difficult access has been Cadgwith's gain, keeping it reasonably unspoiled, a diminutive stone gem above a tiny beach. Coverack, a few miles north up the Lizard's eastern coast, also stone and thatch, has a better road allowing intrusion, and has lost character. This is the epitaph for so many Cornish coastal villages.

Constantine, at the head of a creek on the north side of the Helford river, enjoys a hillside setting with fine views to the south, and is named after a saint. Nearby granite quarries explain its size and provided the stone for its houses, although many are of slate. Some larger houses have stone mullions, a

Mousehole

comparative rarity for this part of Cornwall, while north of the village is a good example of a fogou, unhappily called Pixie's Hall, whose subterranean passages are lined with granite walls.

Slate having been mentioned here as a building material, it seems sensible to say something about it now, especially as it occurs in England in very much the same areas as granite. Whereas granite is an igneous rock with a crystalline structure, slate is metamorphic, formed by the action of great heat or pressure, or both, acting on existing rocks to change their nature and composition. Usually it is the shales and clays close to the volcanic masses and lava flows of the granite regions which have been baked or compressed into slates, and as the pre-existing rocks were of different colours so are the resultant slates.

Slate's greatest characteristic is its cleavage ability, allowing it to be split naturally along parallel planes. This has resulted in its having been used for centuries for roofing, paving, steps, shelves, water-tanks, fences, and, at the end of the day, for gravestones. More recently its use as a cladding material for modern structures of steel and concrete as well as for domestic furnishings and household items ensures that, in some parts of Britain, slate-quarrying is a continuing prosperous industry.

When used as a building material it is called slate-stone, occurring naturally as sizeable lumps in screes beneath rock-faces. Slate-stone is also quarried, but the material is very rarely used in buildings beyond the areas where slate naturally occurs. Because, like granite, it is usually dark coloured, its dour appearance is often lightened with colour-wash. Individual stones are often only roughly dressed, and are naturally long and thin, sometimes narrowing almost to a point, so, although slate-stone masonry is coursed, it does require much more mortar than a wall of good squared stonework. Buildings in exposed situations frequently have slates hung vertically on their more vulnerable walls to give extra protection from Atlantic gales.

In 1790 Sir Charles Rashleigh, of Menabilly, asked John Smeaton to design and build a small port near St Austell where cargoes of china clay could be despatched and coal brought in. Wharves, warehouses, and a whole new settlement were built, the result of enterprise and late eighteenth-century planning, and Charlestown, today, is a charming slate-stone village, with colour-washed cottages above the harbour. As with so many other Cornish villages the stone is hidden, yet you know it is there.

So, too, at Polperro, further along the south coast, undeniably attractive, a collage of cottages above a boat-bobbing harbour, a tangle of narrow lanes and a mish-mash of signs. The best view is from the harbour entrance, with hill-climbing houses and slate roofs reflected in the water, and unattractive new developments up the valley hidden from view.

Across the peninsula to the north coast, Port Isaac cascades in a rhythm of roofs to a cliff-guarded bay. Pairs of double-yellow lines are an idiot outrage in streets so narrow and steep, upper floors overhang thick bulging walls, slate-hung dormers give views on to grey slate roofs, walls are white-washed,

Delabole, Cornwall. Colour-washed Delabole slate; slate roofs and slate-stone chimney stacks

doors and window-frames black or pale blue, and geraniums brighten flights of steps. A fine warehouse by the harbour is the working headquarters of Port Isaac's shell fishermen.

Nearby, Port Gaverne's natural rock-cut quay was exploited last century for exporting huge quantities of Delabole slate, brought laboriously from the famous quarry 5 miles (8km) north-east. England's biggest hole in the ground is 400ft (122m) deep and over a mile (1.6km) round, a huge chunk of scenery destroyed, yet an awe-inspiring piece of landscape created over four centuries. In Delabole and nearby villages, the hard but light Delabole slate, grey or blue-green, is used for all buildings, dressed for walls, thin-sliced for porches and lintels and roofs, but as thick slabs for paving. Older cottages have upper windows close to the eaves so that there is no heavy weight on lintels, lower windows being protected by relieving shallow arches of upright slates. Stacks are often squat and slightly pyramidal with projecting courses of slate. Many walls are colour-washed, and, this being a quarrymen's village, neatness is more apparent than prosperity, and the pub reflects the local industry in its name 'Bettle and Chisel'. It makes a change from 'The Ship' or 'The Tinners' Arms'. Opposite the quarry entrance a row of miniature houses demonstrates the colour and quality of the range of Delabole slate.

Tintagel's euphonic name and its association with Arthurian legend are scarcely matched by its appearance. The village of slate-stone houses has been swallowed by the tourist tides, and insensitive development since last century has destroyed all character, except for one building, the Old Post Office. One room in this former fourteenth-century manor-house was thus used from 1844 to 1892, and the name has stuck. This rare surviving medieval house of dark stone with tiny windows and a heavy slate roof and chimney-pots made of four edge-set slates is now in the care of the National Trust. One swallow may not make a summer, but this building does redeem an otherwise undistinguished village.

Along the northern coast, Boscastle, equally popular with visitors, lacks the legends but savours the slate. Houses and cottages by the north side of the walk to the harbour grow from the slaty bedrock, some proudly naked, some clothed in colour-wash. Grey-green roofs of Delabole slate catch and reflect the western light; walls of upright slates embank the lively stream and pattern the curving breakwaters, where the tide's rise and fall creates fresh shapes and colours. Rock-cut steps or slate ramps, sky-grey and worn, lead down to the water. A tiny, slate-domed shelter crouches into a hillside, and bright veins of quartz shine among the contorted dark slate near Profile Rock.

*(opposite)*_____

Plate 7 Grange-in-Borrowdale, Cumbria. Superb setting in Borrowdale. Cottages of colour-washed slate, but the church keeps its green slate naked in angular beauty. Graceful two-arched bridge spans the clear green Derwent

Altarnun, Cornwall. Cottages of dark brown stone and slate; little colour-wash

Bodmin Moor is the most distinctive area of Cornish granite, a miniature Dartmoor translated beyond the Tamar. Tumbled tors break the skyline above deep wooded valleys, and winding lanes link scattered lonely farms. Villages grew from 'church-towns' on the moorland edge, and Altarnun, just off the traffic-torn A30, is one of the best. Sitting snugly in the sheltered valley of the Penpont Water and reached only by deep, sunken lanes, Altarnun is a single street of cottages, granite and slate-stone in their walls, with granite quoins and occasionally granite lintels and string-courses, browns and dark-grey. White woodwork, sometimes a colour-washed front or gable, and the odd slate-hung wall, harmonise to show as good a village scene as Cornwall can offer. All roofs are slate, some cement-slurried.

At the bottom of the street a pair of stone cottages with granite lintels and door-case overlooks a packhorse bridge, and across the stream, above a high flowered bank, stands the huge parish church of pale grey stone, unusually dedicated to St Nonna, mother of the patron saint of Wales. Celtic saints and slate seem to go together.

*(opposite)*_____

Plate 8 Crovie, Grampian. Colour-washed cottages on a narrow, tapering ledge above the shore seen from above, a pattern of roofs, gables and chimneys

Blisland

Polyphant, a few miles east of Altarnun, merits mention if only because it gave its name to an unusual stone quarried locally, a dark grey-blue stone, sometimes brown-spotted, and occasionally used in church tracery. Mature trees give the hamlet a sylvan appearance, and two rows of cottages show dark rubble walls probably of this material.

St Breward is a string of small hamlets along the western edge of Bodmin Moor, high above the wooded valley of the River Camel. Open moorland runs down to the back of the village, where austere granite cottages have little shelter from the winds that sweep across the plateau, or from the distant sea. By contrast, hill-perched Blisland to the south, sheltered by mature trees, unusually for Cornwall, enjoys the advantages of a large green where some ash and sycamore survive and young ones are thriving. All around is the granite from the moor, in cottages on the north side, by the churchyard entrance on the south, as window-dressings, as chimney-stacks, and most beautifully in The Mansion House, newly restored on the eastern edge of the green. Lumpy granite blocks in its walls, rough-hewn granite quoins, simple lintels, and Swiss-roll finials above the two-storeyed porch, show local stone in its best secular use.

Below the green, Blisland's church, euphonically dedicated to St Proteus and St Hyacinth, hangs on its hillside, unprepossessing in the outer view, breathtakingly beautiful inside – blue slate and pale stone on the floor, a blue-grey arcade of lilting granite columns above, carved benches of dark oak, white walls, and a riot of coloured woodwork in rood-screen and loft, golden altars and rich stained glass. This and the woodwork are relatively new, 1897, a superb evocation of the medieval past, a brilliant and glorious oasis of colour at the granite heart of a grey, bleak landscape. The contrast makes Blisland a stone village of pilgrimage.

Luxulyan, Cornwall. A holy well, granite-built, in a granite courtyard, with grey granite houses in the village street beyond

Luxulyan's name raises hopes of something rather special and the village does not disappoint, expecially if approached from the south by the narrow winding road along the valley. Luxuriant vegetation clothes steep hillsides, strewn with granite boulders, and the spectacular Treffry Viaduct strides across on giant granite legs. The road rises to the hillside village, to houses of roughly coursed grey granite blocks. Gable-end chimneys add solidity, and smaller slabs of granite set upright together make shaped lintels. Stone steps lead to houses at different levels up the village street, or down to the granite-cobbled courtyard of the Holy Well, newly restored, its own granite clean, slab-roofed, and surrounded by high walls of fine-grained black-and-white granite.

Cyclopean blocks form the base of the church tower, one quoin measuring over 8ft (2.4m) long by 2ft (0.6m) deep, while the coffin slab at the lychgate is even longer. Fine-cut slate headstones, with deeply incised lettering, so characteristic of many Cornish churchyards, set the contrasting seal on a splendour of hard stone.

In Cornwall's south-eastern corner, St Germans overlooks its harbour almost ½ mile (0.8km) away, proud of having the county's greatest church until Truro Cathedral was built. Landrake quarries provided the blue-green elvan stone for its superb western portal, but in the village itself the restored seventeenth-century almshouses with slate-hung gables above timber balconies reached by granite steps form the main interest. However, 100yd (91m) away, along a cul-de-sac, a pair of double-fronted small-gabled cottages have brown, buff and grey-green stones in their walls, and blue-green elvan stone in their lintels, a rare domestic use of this attractive stone.

Cornwall's granite occurs in four areas throughout the county, but that of Devon is concentrated in one huge chunk. Dartmoor is England's largest single area of granite, but because of the reasonable availability of a variety of more suitable building stones, its granite was not extensively quarried until the early years of last century. It was used in the fourteenth century for quoins and buttresses of churches, and in the following century for arcades and window tracery. When the rebuilding of manor-houses and farmhouses began in late Tudor times, moorstone was widely used on and around Dartmoor and finely dressed granite can be seen in these buildings today. When smaller houses were rebuilt in later years, granite was used, more as rubble, and frequently colour-washed.

Devon is not a county of large, fully blown villages of the type which is common over much of England, and the villages around Dartmoor's edge are, for the most part, little bigger than hamlets dignified by a solidly squat granite church, grey and unpretentious. Most villages are on the northern and eastern edges of the moor, including the oldest, Grimspound, 1,500ft (457m) up in a fold of hills by Hameldown Tor, west of Manaton. Twenty-four small round huts spread over 4 acres (1.6ha) are enclosed within a boundary wall of 6ft

Throwleigh, Devon. Massive granite blocks in a cottage by a lychgate

(1.8m) high and 9ft (2.7m) thick, of huge granite boulders with rubble infill. A stream flows through the northern part of the enclosure, and entrance to the pound is by a paved passage through the wall thickness. Huts are between 9ft (2.7m) and 15ft (4.5m) in diameter, rough-walled with granite to about 3ft (1m), with granite door-jambs and hearths. Grimspound was a late Bronze Age village of pastoral farmers, the best known of a number of 'pound' settlements on Dartmoor.

Granite churches are the focal points of Dartmoor's villages, where whitewashed rendering too often disguises the hard stone of cottage walls, diluting the granite ethos. At Drewsteignton, from the little square you enter the churchyard by a lychgate tucked against the front of a small almshouse whose gable shows granite blocks bigger than panes of glass in its tiny windows. High above the wooded Teign valley to the south-west, Lutyens' arrogant Castle Drogo, not completed until 1930, is the last great country house likely to be built in England, a final gasp of granite pride and cool austerity.

Threading lanes west of the A382 lead to Gidleigh and Throwleigh at the heart of their secretive and beautiful parishes. Each has a handful of plump, thatched cottages, one or two revealing their textured stone, where roses and clematis colour and soften the rough surfaces, and butterflies bask in summer sun. On the main road, Moretonhampstead has the busy function of a town but retains villageyness, and deserves inclusion if only for the sake of its remarkable almshouses. This long, low building of 1637 has an open colonnaded ground floor adjoining the road, with stumpy columns of granite, a continuous lintel above the arches, and a wall of huge squared granite blocks with three tiny windows beneath wide eaves and a thatched roof. Although gables are of rubble, the whole building represents a remarkable achievement in such a hard stone, at so early a date. Many small manors and farmhouses, also of seventeenth-century date, can still be seen around the edges of Dartmoor, usually in isolation, occasionally – as at Chagford, Poundsgate, Ponsworthy and a number of other small towns and hamlets – of roughly dressed granite, with only the simplest decoration. But there is scarcely a Dartmoor village where every house and cottage bares all, so to speak.

Lustleigh beckons, pleases in its groups, but disappoints by its intrusions of brick and Victorian half-timbering. Most of Manaton's cottages round its wedge-shaped green hide their stone beneath white colour-wash. Much closer to the heart of the moor, and reached by moorland roads passing gaunt, craggy tors above hillsides of hedged fields, Widecombe-in-the-Moor shows more granite character than its tourist popularity leads you to expect. Its lofty church tower beckons in the valley of the East Webburn river. Interesting buildings are grouped around its small square, a sixteenth-century church house, with portico, a glebe house of the same century, and the Old Inn, all of them of unadorned moorstone, with roofs of slate. By contrast, Buckland-in-the-Moor's sylvan setting and more silvery granite houses with snug thatch and generous overhangs, seems the archetypal Devon village. It almost comes up to expectations, the better for being in three separate groupings, the best being in the valley bottom where granite and thatched cottages are neighbourly across a rocky stream.

Leicestershire seems an unlikely place for granite, yet between Dartmoor and Cumbria it is the only English county where it has been quarried, though

Woodhouse Eaves, Leicestershire. Swithland slate and quarry rubble in Charnwood Forest

more for road metal than for building stone. Observant motorists on the M1 will see bare outcrops where the road cuts through the ancient rocks of Charnwood Forest south-west of Loughborough, and the retaining walls of the embankments are made of some of Britain's oldest rocks. The granite was quarried at Mountsorrel, 6 miles (9.6km) north of Leicester, but only since about 1820, when new methods of cutting this very hard stone became available. Before then it had been used, as random rubble, for cottages, farmhouses and boundary walls.

Associated with the granite, however, is the far more important Swithland slate, quarried during Roman times as a roofing material, and from the thirteenth century until 1887, when the last quarry closed, as a material for roofs, walls, headstones, and, by the end of the eighteenth century, for cottages. All Charnwood slate, from Swithland, Groby or Woodhouse Eaves, is dark, usually blue-grey, sometimes green-tinted, and acceptable to moss and lichen. As a slate-stone for building, it is best seen in a fine row of cottages at Woodhouse Eaves. Their dark rubble walls, triangular gabled dormers and shared doors, white-framed latticed windows, and tall clustered chimneys above a long slate roof, are beautifully offset by long front gardens.

Smaller groups and individual houses of slate-stone occur throughout this village and also at Swithland itself, an estate village of 1830–40, with the best examples on the south side of a single long street, Some house walls contain both slate and granite, and a tiny conical-roofed turret behind a garden wall is of granite. Slate is used for all roofs, garden and roadside walls which, with the wooded remnants of Charnwood Forest, brackeny hills and knobbly outcrops, impart an elemental, more northern overtone to this Midland county.

Strong fences now ring the deep, water-filled slate-quarries in Swithland Wood, disused for almost a century. The slate itself was used most decoratively for headstones. Any churchyard in the district illustrates this. Oldest headstones at Swithland, Woodhouse Eaves, Groby, and particularly at Breedon-on-the-Hill, show crude lettering of pre-eighteenth-century date, but during Georgian times masons had perfected a fine, flowing script, with superbly elegant lettering of wide variety, occasionally with low-relief carving added. Headstones of Swithland slate, identifiable as having one side rough, are some of the most beautiful ever produced, and were used throughout Leicestershire and its neighbouring counties.

Cumbrian granite occurs on the edges of the Lake District, at Shap on the east and around Eskdale on the south-west. Only in the Eskdale area has it been used for building, principally in field walls and barns, where pale-pink river boulders give added distinction to this most beautiful of Lakeland valleys. This is an area of scattered farms and tiny hamlets rather than villages, but seen from the lower slopes of the hillside to the north, where haematite was quarried in huge quantities last century, the clustered cottages, restored mill, and packhorse bridge at Boot, comfortably clustered, make a memorable picture.

Slate-stone, and a backcloth of majestic but friendly hills, gives villages in the Lake District their unique character. Colours range from sombre greys, grey-browns, blacks, purples, tawny, to the superb green slate from Langdale and Honister, so there is always variety. When used in house walls, slates are either quarry waste, identified by their unevenness and angularity, or roughly quarried lumps, or taken from screes or stream beds. Elterwater in Langdale is a quarrymen's village, and because of the glorious sea-green stone, colourful to a degree not shared by any other village. Only a few houses have been rendered and lime-washed; the rest show beautiful naked stone. Enormous lintels, irregular in shape, and massive uneven quoins, all from quarry waste, contrast in size and colour with thin, dark slates of walls. If mortar is present it is recessed so deeply as to be invisible. Even where modernised, window-openings are small, chimney-stacks are small, and roof slates are laid in diminishing courses. Knobbly rocks break the surface of small greens amid the grass and bracken of Elterwater Common. Westwards is the most familiar and

(opposite)——————————————————————————————
Boot, Cumbria. Granite in the mill building on the left, whitewashed in the village street

Elterwater, Cumbria. Cottages of green slate quarry waste. Note the enormous slate lintels

Elterwater

exciting mountain profile in England, where the twin Langdale Pikes dominate the valley head 4 miles (6.4km) away.

Chapel Stile, a mile (1.6km) up the road from Elterwater village, squats uneasily beneath Raven Crag, with Thrang a dramatic reminder of the harsh beauty of quarried rock, and village houses seem merely a logical and more ordered extension of it. A tortuously exciting road snakes across the hill to Grasmere, reached more easily by the main road north from Ambleside. Gone is the pure green stone of Langdale, and instead purple-grey tints predominate in the rather stylish late-Victorian villas and small boarding-houses. Wordsworth's one-time home, Dove Cottage, is rendered and whitewashed, but the simple headstone above the poet's grave in Grasmere churchyard is honest slate.

Troutbeck spreads itself for a mile (1.6km) along the east side of the valley which carries the main road from Windermere to Patterdale and Ullswater. Fortunately, this misses the village which is really a string of hamlets, each centred on a spring or well, and with the church ½ mile (0.8km) away Troutbeck has no nucleus. But it does have fine buildings, many of bare slate-stone, some rendered and whitewashed, like Town End at the southern end of the village. This remarkably unaltered house of the Brownes, a well-to-do yeoman family, dates from 1623 and remained as the family home for over three centuries. The house has belonged to the National Trust since 1948, a superb example of Cumbrian vernacular building, its furniture, books and fabric uniquely evoking the life of Lake District 'statesmen' through the generations. Opposite is the barn, of unrendered slate, a bank barn with deep projecting wings and its door canopy extended as a gallery. Over one mullioned, unglazed window is a 1666 datestone.

A walk through the village reveals a succession of surprises. Most houses are on the east side facing across the valley with their backs to the village street. Farms and their bank barns form small enclaves, frequently built at right angles to each other. Quarry waste was commonly used in the mid-eighteenth century, especially for barns and small cottages. When the railway reached Windermere in 1847, new houses were built for Lancashire merchants, the two inns rebuilt for visitors, and the village acquired much of its present appearance. Recent restoration has revived derelict property, but the slaty character survives. Some farm buildings retain wooden mullions in windows, North Fold even having an oriel and a barn with a spinning gallery. Many houses have cylindrical chimneys, sometimes on corbelled projections from gables, and at the group around High Fold one barn has crow-stepped gables. A canopied bank barn near The Mortal Man has limestone quoins, but slate is predominant, especially on roofs. Slate-stone drinking troughs for horses formerly using the Kirkstone Pass add to the symphony of slate in this unique village created by farmers, spinners, weavers and quarrymen.

In northern Lakeland, Braithwaite, near Keswick, is a huddle of houses,

Watendlath

almost all of slate-stone hidden beneath white rendering, but Grange-in-Borrowdale merits inclusion for its remarkable little Victorian church with its spiky, slaty window arches, walls of subtly coloured slates, and upright slate slabs as fencing. The village also has a superbly graceful two-arched bridge spanning the clear River Derwent whose waters reflect the green hillside beyond, so that water, stone and hills show the whole tonal range of green. Southwards, the grey-green stone of Borrowdale's villages is often hidden beneath rendering and white-wash, but Stonethwaite, just off the main valley road, is a tiny gem beneath frowning crags, while hidden among the hills above Rosthwaite is Watendlath, reached by a tortuous lane along a rare upland valley behind Grange Fell. Hugh Walpole's 'Herries' novels were set there and laid the tourist trail. But the best approach, for the energetic, is by the steep pony-track from Rosthwaite, with its unforgettable views of Borrowdale, and equally rewarding ones of Watendlath's few farms, cottages, packhorse bridge, tarn, enfolded by hills.

Neither Hawkshead nor Coniston, good villages both, enjoy the purity of slate unadorned, for rendering and whitewash hide most of the house walls. You know the slate is beneath, but you see it only on the roof, occasionally in lintels. Hawkshead's heart reveals its former status, a tiny market town, a warren of snug squares linked by alleyways, with cobbled pavements, quiet courtyards, and covered ways beneath canopied porches. Many cottages have outside stairs, some have spinning galleries, some have slate-hanging. Sunlight dances on walls, shadows spring out from pillars and porches. Hawkshead is a village of corners and angles, surfaces and shapes, tones and textures, a delight of light and shade.

By contrast, Broughton-in-Furness is grey. Still of slate, but of a dark grey, unifying walls and roofs, so that it is scarcely surprising that most of the buildings round its broad, stately square choose to protect and brighten their walls with rendering and colour-wash, usually white, sometimes cream, with woodwork picked out in black or a bright colour. A stone drinking trough, trees, and an obelisk marking George III's jubilee in 1810 add to the atmosphere of quiet calm which characterises this village beyond the southern fringe of Lakeland.

Stonethwaite, Cumbria. Local slate stone; note the huge lintel over the near window, only partly obscured by whitewash

9
Wales

Wales is a land of scenery and song rather than of stone villages. Although most of its traditional buildings are of stone, the rural and pastoral economy which has dictated its ways of life through many centuries has produced a landscape of hundreds of small farmhouses and crofts, usually isolated, occasionally grouped into hamlets, but rarely clustered into villages. Only in some coastal areas, or where there has been a strong English influence such as in south Pembrokeshire and the Vale of Glamorgan, as well as along the Border country, do nucleated villages occur to any marked extent.

The rocks which have produced Snowdonia's dramatic mountain landscapes and the spectacular cliffs and headlands of the south-west are largely granites and slates. Silurian slates of great age are also responsible for the lonely sheep-voiced uplands of mid-Wales, heavy with memories of droving days. Sandstones in the Vale of Clwyd in the north and the Vale of Glamorgan in the south yield better quality farmland and more prosperous looking settlements. Pennant sandstones have created the flat-topped moors above the coalfields of the South Wales valleys, and during the last century were the principal material used to construct the monotonously dull, grey terraces of miners' houses which line the valleys and climb the hillsides. Although pockets of limestone both in the north and south provide scenic contrasts and bright green fields, they have not influenced building forms. There are no rocks of the Jurassic period responsible for giving us the finest English buildings, and this is one of the chief factors in the poorer quality of village architecture in Wales. Nevertheless, there is a variety of rocks throughout the country and it is surprising that this is not reflected in the houses of Welsh villages.

The overall uniformity of Welsh traditional buildings is partly explained by the fact that, unlike most of England, whose great periods of rebuilding occurred mainly in two phases, 1575–1640 and 1670–1750, that of Wales was compressed into a single phase, and took place later, during the late eighteenth and first half of the nineteenth century. Earlier houses, especially those of a modest size, have rarely survived, and there is more consistency of building styles to which is added an even greater uniformity in the use of roofing materials which are mainly slate, occasionally thatch and, regrettably too often, corrugated iron, though this is not so bad when painted black. There is an overall absence of freestone, with no alternative except local stone, usually a dark-brown or grey-brown slaty stone used as random rubble, roughly coursed, with the need for plenty of mortar. In the north and far south-west where granite was available, this produced brighter colours, dark green or red, but, as with the rest of Wales, the tendency has been to render the surface and whitewash or pink colour-wash the walls. Repeated whitewashings over the years has resulted in a gradual accretion of lime over the rough masonry creating a smooth but lumpy appearance which, under sharply angled sunlight, produces an unusual textural effect. This is particularly noticeable in the coastal areas of Anglesey and Pembrokeshire. Throughout Wales a modest simplicity is the rule, with hardly any ostentation or decorative treatment of detail. Date-panels in village houses are a rarity.

When in the mid-eighteenth century Wales' simple rural economy was affected by the Industrial Revolution, improved communications allowed textile manufacture, quarrying and mining to expand. New jobs were created, absorbing not only local labour but English immigrants. New clusters of cottages were added to rural hamlets, soon to be brooded over by vast, four-square chapels which are still the visual focal point of so many villages and small market towns, often dominating a square, a street, or standing in proud isolation in a lonely landscape.

A survey of Welsh stone villages involves selecting representatives from different areas. Gwent embraces much of the Old Red Sandstone country, and between the English border and the Black Mountains is a soft landscape of wooded hills, streams and scattered hamlets. Skenfrith grew up round one of the trilateral castles, a small cosy village of warm-toned sandstone houses, some whitewashed, most with brick window surrounds. Across the road and above a green sward are the castle's sandstone curtain walls, circular towers and keep guarding the river crossing of the Monmow, while at the northern end of the village a huge angled buttress of similar stone supports the massive tower of the church, capped by a two-tiered pyramidal timber belfry.

A few miles north-west, Grosmont's single street has as its focus a small town hall, venerable in appearance yet dated 1902, probably a rebuilding, but illustrating Grosmont's former borough status. Houses and inns of mellow stone, many white-rendered with black-painted dressings, have old-style lamps on wall-brackets, so an attractive street is not disfigured by unsightly posts. Above the street the castle ruins on their motte are distinguished by an exquisitely delicate fourteenth-century chimney constructed, like the rest of the building, of pink sandstone.

Beneath the dramatic north-western escarpment of the Black Mountains, Talgarth's friendly little market square is dominated by a plain Victorian town hall and a medieval tower, like a Northumbrian pele, with a shop built into it and a bank built on to it. Old shop-fronts and advertisements are confronted by a supermarket and its signs on the north side of the square which characterise twentieth-century tastelessness. Behind, the little River Enig rushes over rocky shelves by two- and three-storey buildings, some with bare rubble walls, all slate-roofed.

To the south, where the Usk valley touches the feet of the Black Mountains, accompanied by the beautiful Monmouthshire and Brecon Canal, beneath a limestone escarpment and beechwoods, Llangattock looks across the river to Crickhowell. From Llangattock's small, stone-paved square by a clear stream a narrow street of former weavers' and quarrymen's cottages leads to the church in its circular churchyard. Restoration has tidied and standardised the houses, their bare walls of uncoursed, roughly squared rubble masonry fronting cobbled pavements. The only ostentation is an occasional drip-moulding above a window, and a stone mounting-block survives by the former Old Six Bells inn.

St Fagans, 4 miles (6.4km) west from Cardiff's busy centre, is not only the site of the Welsh Folk Museum in the house and grounds of the sixteenth-century castle but is also a charming village on the hillside between castle and river. Admittedly, its orderliness is contrived, with whitewashed, thatched cottages, some gabled with tiny leaded-light windows, behind stone walls and trim hedges, but planned picturesqueness is not a common quality in Wales so that its rarity value is worth comment.

A similar neatness characterises St Hilary, near Cowbridge, where restrained modernisation of a number of eighteenth- and nineteenth-century

Talgarth, Powys. Rubble-stone and whitewash

houses built of local limestone, with some thatched roofs, produce an unusual 'Englishness' in appearance. So, too, at Merthyr Mawr beyond Bridgend, an estate village of whitewashed cottages casually grouped round a green near an early Victorian church. One has a splendidly corbelled chimney, another an outside stair, and deep 'eyebrows' of thatch almost hide upstairs windows. The public telephone box is embedded in a wall of Candleston Castle park so that it does not upset the harmony, and the River Ogmore nearby is spanned by an unusual medieval bridge with holes in the parapet above its arches through which sheep were pushed into the water to be dipped.

Gower's delights are primarily of seascapes, stunning cliff and coastal scenery, and the flowers and birds associated with it. Villages in its eastern part are growing in size under the influence of nearby Swansea. Winds, waves and weather have carved, cut and gnawed the limestone cliffs, but the same rock yields a poor quality building stone, invariably requiring a protective coating of colour-wash or whitewash, often on a rendered surface. Oxwich is undeniably a stone village in a sheltered setting behind a headland, an attenuated shape being more responsible for its appeal than any outstanding houses, although an occasional thatched roof – most are of slate – and roses round the door add a quota of charm. To the west, the road from Swansea comes to an abrupt end at a short steep hill of whitewashed houses leading down to a sandy beach at Port Eynon.

Further west again, Rhosili's cliff-perched colour-washed cottages face the splendid sweep of Rhosili Bay, where a 3 mile (4.8km) arc of shining low-tide sand is overlooked by the highest land in Gower, the 600ft (183km) high Rhosili Down. Inland, Reynoldston is at the heart of western Gower and compensates for the absence of a sea view by having a generous open green with whitewashed cottages attractively dispersed around it. But here, as throughout much of western Gower, it is in the many miles of field walls that the local limestone reveals its rough naked beauty. In some exposed places these stone walls, built high to give protection from strong westerly winds, curve slightly outwards at the top to try to reduce the wind's force. This is in marked contrast to field walls in other stone areas of Britain where an inward batter is the general rule.

From Gower's western coast to Laugharne is a seagull's flight of 14 miles (22km) less than one-third of the way by road, by Llanelli, Burry Port, Kidwelly and Carmarthen. Laugharne has withstood the pilgrim pressures attendant on a small town or village with fame thrust upon it by a quirky genius who wrote his famous play for voices there. But the 'Llaregyb' of Dylan Thomas' *Under Milk Wood* seems far more than a generation distant from present-day Laugharne. Many three-storey late Georgian houses, mostly rendered and colour-washed, elegantly line King Street still dominated by the 1746 clock-towered town hall whose steeple-borne golden rooster looks down on roofs of Welsh slate. Houses of mellow red stone in Duncan Street, and

169

cottages in Water Street and around The Grist are more in keeping with the fishing-village image, complemented by cobbled back lanes and a riverbank walk with views to the stone castle and the white-balconied Boat House from which Dylan Thomas retreated to write in the blue-painted wooden cabin above the tidal estuary, ironically almost the only non-stone building in Laugharne.

The Ordnance Survey Sheet 158, 'Tenby', shows not only the pattern of scattered settlements linked by miles of winding lanes, and an absence of nucleated villages, but suggests the counterpane countryside of gentle hills watered by quiet rivers and streams, with modest whitewashed farms in every view, so characteristic of south-western Wales. Narberth, just off the A40, grew beneath the protection of its late Norman castle, now ruined, subsequently developed as a market focus for a large area, and acquired a railway station. Georgian and Regency houses, rendered and colour-washed, are rather more elegant than may be expected in rural Wales and give an urban character to the place.

Pembrokeshire is to Wales what Cornwall is to England and the Mull of Galloway to Scotland, a remote, windswept peninsula with the sea on three sides, a magnificent coastline of contorted cliffs but few small sandy bays and beaches, light of a clear intensity, and stone. Stone in the field walls which stitch the plateau, stone in the prehistoric remains and ruined villages of the far south-west, stone in the volcanic outcrops of the north and on the Preseli Hills, stone beneath the whitewash of farms and cottages.

Pembrokeshire's southern part is the 'Little England' where, for the tourist, it is a map-reader's relief to find English place-names, but a traveller's disappointment to visit a series of undistinguished villages. Too frequently it is only a single building that merits attention, as at Manorbier, west of Tenby, completely castle-dominated, and Lamphey with its fourteenth-century Bishop's Palace, extensive ruins in brown and grey stone, ½ mile (0.8km) from a village which has grown round a railway station.

St Florence is far more rewarding, compactly grouped at the centre of a tangle of lanes west of Tenby. In the twelfth century Norman kings encouraged people from Flanders to settle in west Wales, and local street names, Flemish Close and Flemish Court, commemorate this ancient link. So, too, do the remarkable Flemish chimneys of two cottages near the church. These are huge tapering cylinders of grey stone, one free-standing, the other abutting a gable-end, both reaching from the ground to well above roof height. Though dating from the seventeenth century, the style is five hundred years earlier. Gothic-arched doorways of stone and window-sills of slate are accents of bare stone that relieve the clean whitewashed masonry of houses old and new in the village which has apparently succeeded in keeping time at bay.

To the north-west, Carew also has a Flemish chimney, thickly covered in ivy, survivor of the village bakery which ceased in 1927. Opposite are some very low, humble cottages with sliding sash-windows. Colour-washed cottages cluster near the castle entrance on the southern bank of the Carew river, where the beautiful castle ruins are so splendidly seen from across the water, ideally on a very early morning in summer, rose-pink in sunlight. If the tide is full, their reflection in the reed-fringed river doubles the delight as seabirds swoop and call. Down-stream the French Mill, restored in 1972, a rare double-tide mill, occupies an attractive Georgian building.

North and west of the Milford river it is the coastal villages which attract, but do not demand, attention. But it is situation, groupings and the use of colour-wash that are remembered. Two- and three-storey houses on the south side of Dale's sheltered, shingled anchorage sit snugly beneath mature woods. To the north, Broad Haven and Little Haven form a contrasting pair, the latter far more attractive, an object lesson in the use of colour-wash on the cottages of its narrow street.

Almost at the focus of the great arc of St Bride's Bay, Solva has not only the most sheltered anchorage for miles, but is a dual-character village at the head of a drowned valley inlet with only a narrow clearance between fine rocky headlands. Roads swoop down from enclosing hills to the older village by the harbour, where pink-washed cottages and houses line the main street. In a narrow adjoining street, Middle Mill provides tweeds and woollens in a good nineteenth-century stone building, and lime-kilns by the harbour suggest a former thriving export trade. Newer housing speckles the hillside to the west.

Kilvert's description of his arrival at St David's in October 1871 cannot be bettered: 'And so we came to the end of the world where the Patron Saint of Wales sleeps by the Western sea.' There is still a sense of adventure in travelling to it, though not so much as in medieval days when two pilgrimages to St David's were said to equal one to Rome. Beneath much tourism-orientated modern development there yet lurks a village heart, slightly above the site of the cathedral. One main street, a couple of side streets, and an overall impression of modest houses and cottages in subdued hues, grey stone, some whitewash, some beige, a few pink. The cathedral itself, and the ruined Bishop's Palace to its west, are bolder, of purple, lilac-grey, yellow and quiet brown sandstone with green swards and gracious trees, all folded in a gentle hollow which hides all but the tower from a distant view. From the north-west only the pinnacles draw the eye to this place of pilgrimage.

Between St David's and Fishguard, and less than a mile (1.6km) from the coast, Trevine is a village literally on the rocks. Plain, two-storey houses line four streets meeting at a central green which is not really a green but an enormous outcrop of grey, slaty rock with patches of grass here and there. Mathry, 3 miles (4.8km) away, scorns all shelter on its hill-perched site, all grey and beige and colour-wash, and good farmland around.

Nevern, near Newport, reached by a minor road from Fishguard to Cardigan, has deep roots, indicated by a superb Celtic cross near the church

Trevine, Dyfed. Village on the rock. Slate, rendering and colour-wash

porch. Colour-wash obscures the dark slate-stone of its houses clustered round a medieval bridge, with its low parapets and riverside steps, but field and roadside walls of angular slate leave you in no doubt as to the nature of the rock. To the south, the shapely peak of Mynydd Carningli graces the scene, its cairns and hut circles, and the Pentre Ifan burial chamber to the east, stony reminders of a civilisation pre-dating the Celts by over a thousand years.

To the north-east is Cardigan on the north bank of the Teifi, but before crossing the river it is worth taking the minor road to St Dogmael's, a tiered village of Victorian villas and cottages which seems specially to have been designed for retired nautical men last century. Terraces are haphazardly scattered at different levels and angles along the hillsides away from the estuary, grey slate or rendered and whitewashed, but the heart of St Dogmael's is around its ruined abbey, although the actual monastic remains are rather scanty. Across the road below the broad green sward of abbey land friendly ducks and geese enliven a neat, but old mill-pond.

Inland, the few main roads keep to the river valleys of the Teifi, Cothi and Aeron, which drain the sheepy hills. Villages are little more than hamlets with a church. Abergorlech is a riverside village south of Lampeter, with a seventeenth-century bridge spanning the Cothi, giving a good view of whitewashed, slated cottages, and a church hidden behind the pub. Conifers of the Forest of Brechfa darken the hillside behind. Upstream, Pumpsaint's few cottages are almost all of dark, unrendered stone, and across the hill to the east Caeo clusters compactly round its big church. White dressings enliven rendered masonry, one terrace has very prominent drip-moulds with huge numbers over doors, and two large gables are slate-hung.

Eastwards beyond the wooded hills of Caeo Forest, and gloriously situated by the River Gwenlas a mile (1.6km) above its meeting with the Tywi, Cilycwm is a gem by Welsh standards. Small, modestly elegant, two-storey cottages of white and colour-washed stone flank the single street. Small stone bridges span a man-made water-course immediately in front of the houses in a cobbled gutter edged with long narrow stones and cobbled pavements. It was designed to provide water for cattle collected in the village from the surrounding hills before they were driven on their journey to distant markets. A cobbled courtyard graces the Neuadd Arms, white painted with quoins crisply picked out in black, and behind it the fifteenth-century church contains notable frescoes. Set back from the street down an alley opposite the church is the Capel-y-Grou, small, Gothic, pertly pink, and proud of its early associations with Welsh Methodism.

Parallel roads follow opposite sides of the Teifi valley north-eastwards to Tregaron, the minor one on the east passing through Llanddewi Brefi, snug

Llanddewi Brefi, Dyfed. Slate simplicity, probably early nineteenth century

beneath its sheltering hills to the east, a compact knot of short narrow streets of colourful cottages, with a few untreated walls of grey-green slate. The pale greens and creams of the post office are exceptional in a place of subdued tones, brightened with flowers, set amid fields patterned by limestone walls. Beyond Tregaron and its unique raised peat-bog, now a National Nature Reserve, is the sombre but typical Welsh street-village of Pontrhydfendigaid whose churchyard is more interesting than the village. Nearby are the scanty grey stone ruins of St Mary's Abbey, Strata Florida, its lonely setting characteristically Cistercian.

North of the Llanidloes–Aberystwyth road you begin to sense the more dramatic landscapes of North Wales to which the attractive little town of Machynlleth forms a southern gateway. From it a choice of roads leads to Dolgellau, each offering specific rewards, scenically and for stone villages. The coast road, the A493, accompanied closely by the railway, hugs the northern shore of the Dovey estuary, swinging northwards beyond Aberdovey. This sea-front village, which developed as a remarkably elegant resort during late Victorian times, enjoys a southern aspect over shining sands and sea. Bright, clean terraces of two- and three-storey houses line the sun-catching front, and behind them rise steep sheltering hills. Until the railway came late last century, Aberdovey prospered as a port sending wool and slate overseas, but road and rail subsequently brought visitors who liked what they found. Aberdovey is restrained, dignified, but Tywyn, a few miles north, is brashly extravert, saved for me by being the seaward terminus of the Talyllyn narrow-gauge railway which links it north-eastwards to Abergynolwyn about 7 miles (11km) away. A minor road also follows the valley, where field walls are of upright slates standing like lines of uneven dominoes on a flat green floor. Beyond Talyllyn lake, it joins the A487 to Dolgellau, skirting the eastern slopes of Cader Idris. Abergynolwyn is a former slate-miners' village, whose vast abandoned quarries are high up on the hillside to the south. Terraces of dark slate houses line the two intersecting streets best appreciated from the hill-road to the Dysynni valley and Llanegryn. There, a single street of two-storey houses, their walls of lumpy slate rubble fretted with white mortar, frames a valley view to distant hills.

The main road north from Machynlleth winds through a beautiful valley between steep hills, thickly afforested on the western side, and the former trackway and old stations of a narrow-gauge railway across the Afon Dulas on the east. Corris lies off the road, a slate-quarrying village whose great tips of shattered slates resemble natural scree, melancholy yet majestic. Houses and cottages are haphazardly grouped, their masonry thinner, more even, and

---

(opposite)

Corris, Gwynedd. Dark grey-brown slate beneath wooded hillsides. Quoins and dressings of lumpy slate and *(below)* slate fencing in a slate village

coursed, with prominent quoins and light-coloured mortar. Apart from council housing, there is very little rendering or colour-wash, although one or two buildings are half-timbered in the 1930s style; and throughout the village slate roofs are generously sized. Beyond them, frowning hills almost exclude the sky from village views, but trees, woods and tiny gardens soften the austerity so that Corris is far more appealing than many other slate-quarrying villages.

A third and longer way from Machynlleth to Dolgellau, by the A470, follows the pastoral Dovey valley to Mallwyd, where another main road branches off to Welshpool. The tiny village looks westwards across the valley to the commanding hills and pine plantations of the Dovey Forest. Modest whitewashed houses gleam in afternoon and evening sunshine, the view from the river bridge, or better still from the narrow lane on the river's western bank, is a lush and tranquil contrast in tones and textures to those at Corris a few miles away on the other side of the hill.

From Dolgellau there is again a choice of roads northwards, either east or west of the desolate, rocky Rhinog Mountains. The seaward route leaves the impressive Mawddach estuary at Barmouth to take a northward orientation, increasingly diverging from the coastline towards Harlech. Lanes leading to the tiny station at Dyffryn Ardudwy have some of the largest bouldered cottages in Wales, some having only a dozen courses of stones between the ground and the eaves immediately above the upper windows. Boundary walls of stone incorporating huge field-clearance boulders add unity and an impression of sculptured solidity to this village of dark slate-stone above widening coastal marshes to the north.

Both roads from Dolgellau converge at Maentwrog, where early Victorian rebuilding in an almost Alpine setting in the Vale of Ffestiniog has contrived a village more memorable than most in North Wales. The 'maen' element means 'stone', and a 4ft (1.2m) sandstone pillar commemorating Twrog, a local Celtic Christian, stands outside the west end of the church. It was William Oakley, a landowning slate-industrialist in the 1830s, who gave Maentwrog the appearance it has today. Concentrated on one side of a single street, cottages of dark-grey slate cling to the lower slopes of a steep cliff, with flights of steps linking separate groups. One towering block of four storeys shadows a row behind with white-painted window-dressings. Eaves have large overhangs, and roadside walls of small thin slates rise directly from slate outcrops. Maentwrog's tiered houses are a windowed, broken cliff of slate, softened by trees and rhododendrons.

Georgian elegance characterises Tremadog, a few miles west of Maentwrog, planned and built about thirty years earlier. William Maddocks, MP for

(opposite)

Maentwrog, Gwynedd. A close view of some of the estate housing

Maentwrog, Gwynedd. Early Victorian estate housing in grey and grey-green slate

Boston, Lincolnshire, but a Denbighshire man, was an idealist whose aim was to improve south Caernarvonshire around the Glaslyn estuary, by reclaiming land and building roads and harbours on land already reclaimed by 1800, situated beneath a wooded cliff of hard, dark dolerite. Maddocks, hoping that the road westwards into the Lleyn Peninsula to Port Dinllaen would become the route from London via Welshpool, Bala and Tremadog to Ireland, named one street in his new town Dublin Street, forming one arm in the T-shaped plan, the High Street the other arm, and the broad Market Place narrowing to Church Street the long southern leg. Building started in 1805, and by 1810 the town hall, market hall, Maddocks' Arms Hotel, church and chapel had been completed, together with the earliest factory-style woollen-mill in Wales just outside the town. Houses and shops were arranged in neat terraces around the town centre, and most of the simple, effective layout of Tremadog survives today as the best Welsh example of early nineteenth-century planning. The subsequent founding and growth of Porthmadog a mile (1.6km) away as a more successful slate-exporting enterprise during mid-Victorian times led to the fossilisation of Maddocks' inland town, to which Telford's choice of the Holyhead route to Ireland was a contributing factor. Thus, Tremadog remains a village-sized failed town, but one of immense charm and unity. Dignified buildings of dark grey-green slate, their roofs even greener, taking reflected

178

colour from the wooded hillside behind, impose an urbanity emphasised by white-framed, tall Georgian windows and classical details of Maddocks' principal buildings. These show-pieces dominate the market square, but in Dublin Street there is one terrace of squat, humble cottages built with huge blocks of slate-rubble, with 'eyebrow' dormers and simple windows. Presumably, these were the homes of the artisans who did the actual building work in Maddocks' venture.

The Lleyn Peninsula, full of promise and pre-history, is largely a lowland promontory with a few exciting volcanic hills thrusting their outcrops above a landscape of scattered farms, quarry villages and coastal settlements increasingly geared to the needs of visitors from Merseyside and the Midlands. Seascapes and inland views to Snowdonia are bonuses, but the villages are, on the whole, unexceptional. On the north coast Trevor typifies the quarry villages of Lleyn, source of a beautiful pink granite, visually appreciated in headstones in the churchyard rather than in the simple quarrymen's colour-washed cottages. West of the Yr-Eifl quarries high above the sea is the Gwrtheyrn valley at whose mouth are the abandoned terraces and chapel of a former quarry village, decayed but with the possibility of restoration. A rough track from Llithfaen offers the more rewarding approach, but if the remains of an older settlement are preferred the Iron Age fort of Tre'r Ceiri, on Yr Eifl's south-eastern summit, should be visited. Granite walls above the scree and heather enclose the remains of 150 huts probably established just before the Roman occupation of North Wales, forming not only the most impressive

Tremadog, Gwynedd. Georgian elegance of William Maddocks' planned town of the early nineteenth century, beneath frowning cliffs of dark dolerite

prehistoric stone village in Wales but the one with the best panoramic view.

Since the death of St Dubricius in 612, Bardsey Island has been a place of pilgrimage, and the northern road along Lleyn follows the route taken by medieval pilgrims. Clynnog-fawr was one of their stopping-places, a village hallowed by its association with the Celtic St Beuno, who founded a great church there. The present large sixteenth-century building probably occupies the original site of Beuno's cell, the lychgate entrance to its churchyard having huge single-slab lintels 8ft (2.4m) long, with shelves over them, stone seats inside, and a cobbled floor, and the main road nearby is flanked by cottages, mainly whitewashed, a few bare-stoned, to form probably the best of the Lleyn villages.

Snowdonia is mountainous and magnificent, with scenery on the grand scale. Too often it is mysterious, melancholy, brooding and grey, qualities which spill down into its villages, particularly those where slate was once worked. Beddgelert is deeply set in the Aberglaslyn Pass between Moel Hebog to the south-west and the Snowdon range to the north. A luxuriously verdant backcloth of trees, shrubs and bracken is the ideal frame for Beddgelert's houses, small hotels and cottages representing the village response in Victorian times to tourists seeking the scenic splendours of Snowdonia. Slate predominates, dressed and coursed in buildings by the two-arched river bridge, with white-painted woodwork and occasional drip-moulds, but to the

Beddgelert, Gwynedd. Nineteenth-century houses and hotels for visitors to Snowdonia in the Aberglaslyn Pass

north-east is a terrace of cottages whose walls are of enormous blocks of dark, slab slate, only ten courses to the eaves and shallow-pitched roofs. Front windows indicate a one-up, one-down arrangement, and crude drip-moulds copy the fashion elsewhere in this, the most beautiful of the villages of Snowdonia, although Dolwyddelan has a more open setting in the upper valley of the Lledr, surrounded by mountains, in a landscape of forests and sparkling rivers. Here, nature has taken over long-abandoned slate-quarries, and the chief landmark now is the restored rectangular keep of a late twelfth-century castle on a rocky knoll west of the village. Houses of dark slate in the main street parallel to the river are dominated by a large Victorian chapel.

East of Betws-y-coed Telford's Holyhead road, the A5, forms a rough boundary between Snowdonia's mountain landscapes and the softer, though still hilly, countryside of Denbighshire and its moors. Except for its coastal strip where limestone has created some diversity, the Denbighshire landscape is one of slaty rocks and smooth-sided plateaus. Main roads tend to stick to valleys, but once these are left for any of the tortuous winding roads which climb eastwards from the trough of the Conwy valley, or westwards from the Vale of Clwyd, they reveal a landscape patterned by hedged fields and isolated farms. The few villages occupy valley sites, but towards the south even these are reduced to hamlets with an inn, a farmhouse, and one or two cottages.

From Llanrwst in the Conwy valley, where the river is spanned by one of the most elegant stone bridges in Wales, displaying the Stuart arms and the date 1636, the A548 follows an attractive course north-eastwards to join the Elwy valley at Llangernyw, and keeps close company with the river to Llanfair Talhaiarn standing on its south bank beyond another shapely bridge with low arches and big cutwaters. Lining a pleasant square are stone houses, some colour-washed with sandstone dressings introducing a different textural element that comes as something of a relief after so much monotony in villages where the slate is so persistently unremitting.

At the easternmost end of the Elwy valley, where the river joins the Clwyd, St Asaph shares with St David's in the south the distinction of being a cathedral city disguised as a village. Admittedly, the late fifteenth-century cathedral is Britain's most modest, smaller than many parish churches, but its situation at the top of High Street overlooking riverside meadows on the west is a particularly commanding one. Buildings in the High Street are similarly restrained and dignified, cleanly colour-washed in various shades, and include some particularly good shop-fronts not marred by unsightly fascia-boards or garish signs. Visually, St Asaph is a more satisfying village than St David's. Nearby, along the A55 to the west, is the most eye-catching spire in Wales, the 200ft (61m) needle of Bodelwyddan's Victorian church, a remarkable building of white limestone seen best against either an azure summer sky or the darkness of passing storm clouds. Marble decorations inside are even whiter, but the village itself is unexceptional.

Clwyd extends an appendix southwards to take in part of the Berwyns, the most easterly of the mountain ranges of North Wales. Wild, lonely skyline ridges of bare rock rise above wide moorlands. Quick-flowing rivers in steep-sided valleys drain eastwards, some with minor roads running only to valley-heads, only two crossing the hills westwards to Bala. There is no main road between the A5 in the north and the A458 20 miles (32km) away to the south. It is a landscape of long perspectives and subtle details, with the few villages among the foothills to the east.

A dozen miles (19km) west of Oswestry is Llanrhaeadr-ym-Mochnant, a compact village of grey stone cottages grouped round two small squares, with additional small terraces. On the church lychgate is commemorated the fact that, during Elizabethan times, William Morgan the rector, later Bishop of St Asaph, made the first translation into Welsh of the whole Bible, subsequently printed in the year of the Armada, 1588. To the west, in the beautiful Tanat valley, Llangynog's industrial past as a lead-mining and slate-quarrying centre has left scars in the hills and a legacy of modest stone houses, most of them whitewashed, between its two bridges over the Tanat and Eirth rivers. Huge bare boulders in the high wall around the churchyard are vital factors contributing to the stony character of the village dwarfed by the frowning rocks and screes of Craig Rhiwarth to the north.

More distant from the Berwyns, the softer Vale of Meifod in the lower course of the River Vyrnwy provides a pastoral setting for the village that gives

Meifod, Powys. Dark brown slate-stone in random walling, enhanced by white-painted woodwork

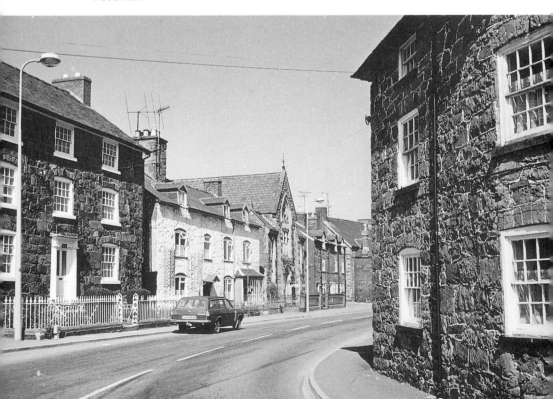

it its name. The A495 keeps to the western side of the valley on a low shelf just above the river's flood-plain, and gives a gentle curving approach to Meifod. An unusually high proportion of three-storey buildings of late Georgian appearance hint at prosperity following the building of a woollen-mill in 1789. White-painted woodwork on doors, window-frames and neat glazing-bars enhance the visual contrast with walls of large dark grey-green stones, coursed, but not spoiled by over-mortaring. Varying heights make an interesting roofscape, with neat gabled dormers imposing their own counterpoint. A Dutch barn at the northern end of the village is supported on lovely, narrowing stone pillars, and overall relatively few buildings are whitewashed. Steep hillsides with mature woodlands are sufficiently distant to create an ideal backcloth to views from the village without enfolding it, so that in setting and in its essential ethos Meifod is as good a stone village as any in this borderland of Wales.

Powys, comprising the former counties of Montgomeryshire, Radnorshire and Breconshire, embraces much of this Welsh border country. Within its landscape of green hills and eastwards-flowing rivers, the settlement pattern of scattered farms and hamlets, with few villages, is typical of most of Wales. But the nearness of England and a general absence of good building stone has resulted in rather more half-timbering than elsewhere. Nevertheless, stone predominates, usually rendered and whitewashed, as at New Radnor, sheltering at the southern foot of the high hills of Radnor Forest. Founded in 1064 to replace Old Radnor as defensive stronghold, it was subsequently planned in late Norman times on a characteristic gridiron pattern, beneath a motte-and-bailey castle mound to the north.

The street pattern survives, with the main A44 passing through the middle, entering from the north-west by High Street near the early Victorian parish church. A row of grey-green stone houses by a raised pavement leads to the right-angled bend southwards into Broad Street. This is the main street of New Radnor but retains little to show its former borough status from 1562 to 1833. At the bottom of the street is a terrace of whitewashed stone cottages of the nineteenth century with a stone Regency house prominent nearby. A clear stream accompanies the parallel Water Street, with small bridges across it leading to houses. As with almost all the Welsh villages visited, there is nothing spectacular or even memorable. The scale is modest with remarkably little individuality of treatment. Of Welsh villages one remembers not the splendour of stone or the craftsmanship of masons but the background beauty of hills or the sea.

10
Scotland

Scotland is essentially a country of stone. Excepting industrial developments of the past century, all villages are stone-built, but, as a glance at the North sheet of the Geological Survey Ten Mile Map reveals, there are none of the oolitic limestones and sandstones which have produced so many memorable stone villages in England. Although there is a similar orientation of strata across the country, patterning it from south-west to north-east, its colours on the map are vivid and bright, with large blobs of red and extensive areas of browns and yellows. The reds and yellows represent rocks of igneous origin, mainly granites, while the brown is the Old Red Sandstone. Across the Border country and the Southern Uplands, the purple bands indicate Silurian slates. While there is no shortage of stone, and many famous quarries have yielded vast quantities of excellent stone, this was mainly used in the eighteenth- and nineteenth-century development of Scottish towns and cities, dignifying streets with handsome buildings of fine ashlar masonry. But throughout rural Scotland vernacular building is remarkably and consistently undistinguished.

For all sorts of cheap walling from the seventeenth century onwards, field stones were readily available almost everywhere, increasingly supplemented by roughly squared material from quarries. These were granites over much of the Highlands and the north-east, mellow red sandstones on the lowlands of the Moray Firth, Strathmore, Angus, Fife, parts of the Lothians, Dumfries and the Borders. In villages throughout these areas, as well as in the rest of Scotland where they are even more scattered, the universal use of stone should make most Scottish villages look extremely dour were it not for the widespread practice of harling. This is the Scottish equivalent of the English roughcast, a surface material consisting of coarse sand, washed gravel, or stone chippings mixed with lime, or more recently, with cement. This aggregate is finely crushed and applied to a wall surface undercoated with lime and sand, or cement and sand, all well moistened at the time of application. Harling produces a continuous weatherproofing coat on the walls, hiding their rough masonry and lime mortar and, in much modern work, breeze blocks and poor quality restoration. Although it imparts unity to the appearance of a building or a whole street, it effectively obscures the local stone. Any available freestone, usually a red or yellow sandstone, is saved up and used for corners and the margins of windows and doorways, or, more exceptionally, for ornamentation such as dated lintels or sculptured trimmings like skewputts – the 'kneelers' at the lower end of gable copings.

Quality and direction of light affects the appearance of a harled surface. With no strong light on it the texture of such a rough surface is dull and uninteresting; with strong sunlight falling directly on it, particularly if it is whitewashed as most harled walls are, its rendered finish is not well revealed but appears as a brilliant but flat white mass. If, however, sunlight glances across a harled surface, or, as in summer months, from a much higher angle in the sky than at other times of the year, each tiny piece of aggregate casts shadow so that the whole harling shows its true, rough texture in subtle detail.

Undoubtedly one of the characteristic details of Scottish stonework in many villages is the crow-stepped gable, a method of finishing off a gable, course by course, as it rises to the roof edge, either on an individual house or at the ends of a short terrace. Probably functional in origin, when gables were rubble-built, crow-steps provided an easy way to climb a roof for repair work or to sweep chimneys, and, if both gables were crow-stepped, narrow planks could be laid along the roof from one gable to the other, making it easier to thatch, tile or slate.

Whitened harl or colour-washed stone doubtless lightens the darkness in the appearance of most Scottish villages but at the same time it reduces their individuality. Scotland's natural landscape is such that the village rarely dominates the scene. You don't visit Scotland for the sake of its villages; you go for its scenery. Against superb background settings of hill and mountain, glen or coast, the ordinary village doesn't stand a chance – although there are one or two exceptions which will be dealt with in due course.

Furthermore, Scottish history has brought about a settlement pattern in the landscape vastly different from that in England, many villages having been developed on new sites, mainly in the eighteenth century, with marked similarities between them.

Before then, and throughout most of the country, the typical unit of rural settlement was the hamlet which in the Lowlands was known as a fermtoun (farmtown) and in the Highlands as a clachan, a Gaelic word meaning 'stones'. These hamlets were the homes of people working together as communities. Occasionally in Lowland Scotland these developed on marginal land and were not affected by eighteenth-century improvements in farming methods which were concentrated on better quality land. Highland clachans rarely survived in their original states because of the sheep clearances of the eighteenth and nineteenth centuries which have left them as deserted settlements identified only by the stone footings of buildings hidden among the bracken and grass in lonely glens.

Some settlements grew with a church and its attendant manse, and often the glebe, or minister's farm, with the church itself situated at a cross-roads or other point conveniently accessible to the people of the fermtouns scattered throughout the parish, of which the resulting kirktoun became the religious centre. Thus, until the early eighteenth century, clachans, fermtouns, kirktouns and, occasionally in the Lowlands, milltouns, formed the characteristic type of rural settlement throughout most of Scotland.

In the south-east, which had been influenced by Anglian settlement, nucleated villages are more common, while some fermtouns grew into villages as they felt the need to exchange their commodities for other essential goods which needed to be brought in from outside the area, so traders and craftsmen moved into former hamlets, particularly in favoured areas of good land and good communications. In the eighteenth century new agricultural methods brought economic and visual changes in rural settlement over much of Scotland, so that, except in the south-east and Fife, the village was a late development and had a completely different function from that of its traditional English counterpart. From 1730 to 1830 new Scottish villages were promoted and planned by landowners anxious to introduce agricultural, industrial or trade developments in order to improve the economy both of their estates and of the Scottish nation. Such villages were also expected to provide a new way of life for people in the countryside, rather like that of English estate villages of the seventeenth, eighteenth and nineteenth centuries. Apart from coal-mining and urban developments, about 150 planned villages were added to the Scottish countryside in the century immediately after the 1745 Rebellion – a good indication of the scale of the 'Improving' movement.

These planned eighteenth-century rural settlements were not, however, a complete novelty in Scotland. A few had been established in the two previous centuries, when some landowners procured charters for burghs of barony, with the aim of compelling smallholders to live together in villages. The more successful of these eventually grew into small towns – Langholm in Dumfries, Newton Stewart in Galloway, Campbeltown in Kintyre, and Stornoway in Lewis. In no sense were these aimed at changing and developing estates as part of the high ideal of promoting growth in the Scottish kingdom, nor did they consider aesthetic and social factors when village appearance was thought out in detail.

Geographically, Scotland's planned villages fall into eight distinct areas, which provide a convenient framework for describing typical examples, but in the broad survey which follows, the older villages, though outnumbered, will not be overlooked. On the ground these can be recognised usually by their more varied house styles, often with older stonework, and a much more irregular street pattern, if one exists at all. They are more at home in their setting than many of the planned villages; they announce their presence in a far more subtle way, and for the most part they are in the south-east – in Fife and East Lothian. Externally, the basic essentials of the planned villages are houses built of freestone with tiled or slated roofs. Many had two, occasionally three storeys, with three to five rooms, and presented a tidy façade.

Sometimes a distinguished architect or his associate was responsible for the ground-plan as well as the house details. William Adam and his son John, with Robert Mylne, planned Inveraray; William's mason, John Baxter, laid out Fochabers, and Telford designed Ullapool and Pulteny town at Wick – although this is not a village but a suburb of the larger town. The simplest plan had two rows of houses facing each other across a wide street, or crossed at right angles, with the main street long, the crossing street shorter and narrower, with a market square or green at the intersection. A large plan was based on an oblong grid which allowed subsequent development to take place in the squares between parallel or intersecting streets. Geometry ruled. In order to avoid untidiness caused by house-occupiers dumping middens in front of their homes, front doors opened directly on to pavements, but long strips of land were provided behind houses, sometimes extending to a couple of acres or more. The resultant absence of a front garden to relieve a long, austere façade is one factor which distinguishes so many Scottish villages from their more flowery English counterparts. Stonework is thus seen at closer range, if it is not harled or colour-washed.

Far to the south on Scotland's western seaboard is the most outstanding of the eighteenth-century planned villages. Like many old royal burghs having the importance of a small town, Inveraray was rebuilt with extreme good taste by the 3rd Duke of Argyll in 1743, and continued its development over the next fifty years. From the north, across an inlet of Loch Fyne, it gives the impression of being, like Venice, borne on water: its distinctive skyline usually seen in silhouette. Linked units on its water-front include an arcaded screen, modest houses, more impressive ones, then the main street of three-storey tenements leading to Mylne's elegant church of 1795 round which the road divides. Stone porticos contrast austerely with harled surfaces all around, but nothing can take away the overall impression of Inveraray being one of the best examples in Britain in which the works of man are so well balanced with those of nature, yet never at the expense of function.

Scotland's oldest stone villages, however, are on the northern isles, Skara Brae, on Orkney, and Jarlshof in the Shetlands. Both have been preserved by wind-blown sand, but as revealed by excavations over the past hundred years, they are the Scottish equivalent of the oldest English stone village at Chysauster, Cornwall, although they differ in showing evidence of occupation over a much longer time. Skara Brae's seven huts, linked by covered stone alleyways, overlooks the Bay of Skaill, and was first inhabited in Neolithic times. By contrast, Jarlshof, not far from the Sumburgh aerodrome, was intermittently occupied from Neolithic to Viking times, its most memorable survivals being the 'wheelhouse' of the second and third centuries, circular stone huts divided into compartments radiating from the centre – an interesting comparison with Chysauser.

Having established a foothold, as it were, in the northern islands, it seems logical to look at the main areas of planned villages starting at the north and working gradually southwards to the Borders. For convenience and personal preference, I propose to stick to the old names of the Scottish counties. In any case, they are more euphonic and less cumbersome than their 1974 successors.

The first group comprises the coastal villages along the shores of Caithness, Sutherland and Cromarty, almost all of which date from 1780 onwards. Caithness' flat, windswept landscape was the most isolated part of the British mainland until it was opened up by Telford's road of 1809 north of Dornoch, now largely followed by the A9. This links most of the fishing villages created by the initiative of two men, Sir John Sinclair of Ulbster, and the 1st Duke of Sutherland, to rehouse crofters from inland glens on their huge estates through the introduction of large-scale sheep farming – the infamous 'clearances'.

Lybster is one of the largest of these settlements, essentially a single broad street running southwards from the main road towards the harbour, dignified by solid stone houses, mainly two-storey, with an impressive hotel at the junction. Flagged pavements with green swards in front help to create a feeling of spaciousness and there is sufficient unharled stone and a variety of roof lines to give a liveliness to the street, whose southern end curves round to a harbour well sheltered by jagged grey cliffs on either side of Lybster Bay.

Lybster, Highland. Sandstone and harling in an eighteenth-century planned layout

Some miles south, at the mouth of the Helmsdale River, is the Duke of Sutherland's gridiron-plan village of 1814. Telford's bridge has been superseded by a modern concrete structure at whose southern end a small park provides a conveniently high viewpoint overlooking the harbour and gives a nice perspective of Helmsdale's parallel streets, neat dormers, slate roofs, and hillside background. Massive squared stones line the harbour wall, and behind the white-fronted cottages and houses along its northern side new building, together with some excellent restoration, has been carried out with care and imagination.

Contrasting with these planned settlements is Dornoch, a royal burgh created in 1628, formerly the county town of Sutherland and once the seat of the bishops of Caithness, although its cathedral is now the parish church. Dornoch's houses in the streets converging on the cathedral are of yellow sandstone, sometimes shading into pink, taking the northern sunlight and giving it back in full measure. Late summer roses climb textured, unharled walls and the two historic buildings in the centre face each other across graceful trees and grassy lawns of the square, decorous and douce as though in reaction to a rather violent history. Sometimes, in spite of increasing numbers of visitors, Dornoch manages to be quiet and peaceful, as well as being dry and sunny when the rest of Scotland is suffering from rain.

Across the Dornoch Firth, 8 miles (13km) distant by water but 36 (58km) by road, Portmahomack, seen in evening sunlight, is a low white arc against the horizon. The closer view shows the haphazard roof lines of a long, shallow curve of cottages along the sea-front, where old anchors protect the base of the sea-wall by Telford's harbour, and at the northern end of the street the crow-stepped gables of a seventeenth-century granary form an eye-arresting accent, its steep roof pitch suggesting an earlier thatch, now replaced by slate.

Similarly remote of access, and at the tip of the Black Isle's jutting finger which so nearly meets the Tain peninsula, Cromarty was once a royal burgh, but by 1672, as a declining port it could not afford to maintain its former status. A century later George Ross, a rich army agent, bought the estate, built a new harbour, established a cloth factory, a lace industry, a spade and nail factory, and a brewery – though not necessarily in that order – and gave the burgh a new Court House complete with tower and cupola (1782) and new merchants' houses in a familiar gridiron pattern of streets. Tightly packed fisher rows border the shore, whose rocks and pebbles of Old Red Sandstone helped to inspire Hugh Miller to a life-long interest in rocks and stones. His white-harled birthplace in High Street, thatched and with tiny upper windows, dating from 1711, is the oldest surviving house in Cromarty (National Trust for Scotland). Miller became a stonemason and his studies of rocks and fossils were subsequently embodied in a geological classic, *The Old Red Sandstone*, published in 1841. For 'stone buffs' Cromarty is a place of pilgimage, meriting inclusion here even though the village is not unduly outstanding.

Black Isle settlements favour the southern coast of the peninsula, with Rosemarkie the best of the villages. Of large, warm-tinted sandstone blocks the houses along its main street have been less obscured than most by harling and occasionally their mortar-courses are enlivened by galletting, perhaps an instinctive appreciation of the need to introduce small detail into surfaces of massive, well-dressed stone. The effect is undeniably attractive, yet is much less used in neighbouring Fortrose, where the presence of a ruined cathedral graces a smooth green sward, surrounded by late eighteenth-century houses.

The second group of planned villages lies in the counties of Moray, Banff and north-west Aberdeenshire, but some older villages have survived. Fochabers was a burgh of barony strategically placed where the highway from Aberdeen to Inverness crosses the River Spey at its lowest bridging-point. The old settlement stood in the way of extensions to Gordon Castle so, in 1770, the Duke of Gordon resited it a mile (1.6km) away, giving it a new, impressive plan in the form of a rectangle bisected lengthways from east to west by the main road. A large market square on this axis is dominated by the elegant parish church of Bellie, 1798, with portico, spire and flanking house-fronts of fine sandstone masonry, a focus for the disciplined terraces of mainly two-storey houses of a more rubbly stone, sometimes harled, which were added during the next three decades.

(above) Archiestown, Grampian. Coursed sandstone, with decorative galletting with small stone pieces in vertical joints and *(opposite)* Portmahomack, Highland. Crow-stepped gables and colour-wash at the tip of the Tain peninsula

Higher up the Spey valley is Archiestown, one of a number of planned villages taking its name from its promoter, in this case Sir Archibald Grant of Monymusk, 1760, but largely rebuilt after a fire in 1783. Small, but also axial along a road, its lines are broken by small greens and trees, softening the cool austerity of the stone houses, some of which show galletting with four or five small rectangular pieces of stone inserted into the vertical joints, creating a lively chequered effect, and one which characterises a number of buildings in the north-eastern counties.

Grant also rebuilt Monymusk at the heart of his home policies about 1750 to house estate workers and craftsmen, with the village enjoying another remodelling at the end of last century, when the older cottages were given an extra storey, their thatched roofs replaced by slate, but the granite houses bordering an elongated green left largely unaltered. The parkland setting is continued within the village with sycamores and silver birches while on the nearby hills extensive larch forests are a reminder of the introduction of this species by landowners like Grant and the Duke of Atholl in the middle years of the eighteenth century.

The north-facing coastline of the Moray Firth eastwards from Nairn has a succession of new or developed fishing villages. Findochty is one of the earliest, founded by fishermen from Peterhead in 1716, but retaining at its heart a winding street of brightly painted rubble-walled cottages, their quoins and

Inverallochy, Grampian. Parallel sandstone terraces of fisher-cottages, gable-ended to the sea

Crovie

dressings picked out in contrast. Nearer the shore are rows of gables at the seaward ends of parallel, single-storey terraces, overlooked by a granite kirk on a higher green. East of Fraserburgh Inverallochy shows even more distinctively this protective plan of cottage rows, gable-ended to the sea, gable-ended to the street, a rhythm of terraces and triangles in diminishing perspective.

Alexander Garden of Troup was the first eighteenth-century landowner to promote fishing villages on this coast, founding Gardenstown and Crovie about 1720. Here the Old Red Sandstone displays superb cliffs to the north but allows only a few breaches where settlements could be established. Approached only by breakneck hairpins, Crovie's cottages occupy a narrow, tapering ledge, the end ones facing the sea, those in the middle in parallel rows, sometimes with two storeys but usually one, running to the base of the cliffs behind. Gardenstown is larger with a more tumbled appearance, where cottages cling tenaciously to any flat space available above the harbour, and, among all Scottish fishing villages, it has become one of the most prosperous. Half its population are Plymouth Brethren, so it has less of a holiday-cottage syndrome than either Crovie or Pennan.

A few miles inland from Portsoy, itself an outstanding example of practical conservation in what may be regarded as a 'fisher-town' rather than a village, with handsome stone buildings near the harbour, Fordyce is an older, unplanned village grouped loosely round the nucleus of the ruined old kirk of St Tarquin and the tiny, elegant sixteenth-century castle where streets meet. Sandstone cottages, grey rather than red, line narrow lanes, and the occasional use of granite, plus roofs of warm-toned pantiles, make for visual charm – not the commonest characteristic of Scottish villages in the north-east.

The third group of planned villages is small – inland settlements in the Central Highlands of which the earliest, Crieff, has grown into an important town. Grantown-on-Spey, now one of Speyside's important resorts and tourist centres, was planned by Sir James Grant in 1766 and still shows characteristic late Georgian spaciousness, overlaid by Victorian urbanity. By contrast, Tomintoul, 12 miles (19km) to the south-east and the highest village in the Highlands (1,160ft (353m)), founded by the 4th Duke of Gordon in 1779, undeniably retains its village size and character. One long single street has a square in the middle with a neat, rather formal green. Houses are mainly two-storey, of either the local limestone or a sandstone from nearby, all slated from the Knockfergan quarry, and built by three generations of stonemasons of the same family. Gabled dormers break the roof lines, but again the absence of front gardens contributes to a sober austerity of appearance. Contemporary planned villages along the Spey valley include Kingussie and Newtonmore, but these lack the distinction of Tomintoul.

Kenmore, at the eastern end of Loch Tay, is one of the few Scottish villages that can be described as charming. It is also one of the few planned villages having an obvious link with the estate of its developing landlord. Founded by the Earl of Breadalbane in 1760, its whitewashed cottages with trellis porches and well-kept gardens indicate an 1840 rebuilding in the 'picturesque' manner, creating a remarkably unScottish scene outside the gates of Taymouth Castle, especially when viewed from the churchyard entrance.

Planned settlements in the fourth group comprise coastal villages along the western seaboard, mostly founded after 1780. From Cape Wrath to Ullapool

Portsoy

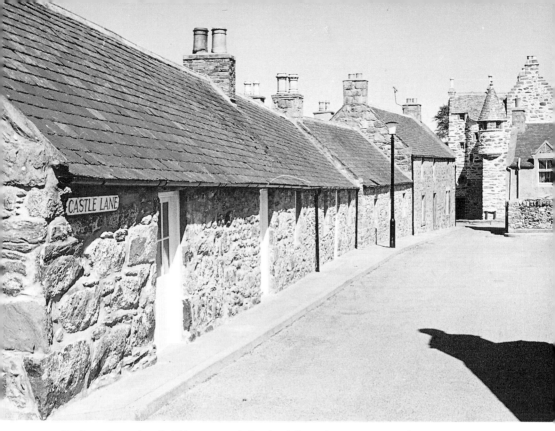

Fordyce, Grampian. Rubble-stone and slate in eighteenth-century vernacular

only Kinlochbervie and Lochinver merit mention, both primarily dependent on fishing, though Lochinver enjoys an increasing tourist trade. Both have sheltered harbours fronted by whitewashed houses, Lochinver's north-facing front having the added dignity of a few hotels, but when seen from across the estuary the village is still dominated by the distant profile of Suilven.

Ullapool was one of four settlements founded and developed by the British Fisheries Society in the late eighteenth century (the others were Pulteneytown in Wick, Loch Bay on Skye, and Tobermory on Mull). Telford's original proposals for Ullapool were far more grandiose than eventually was the result, a rectilinear plan, with lanes crossing by garden walls. The village has a double-sided frontage to Loch Broom, its peninsula site ideally appreciated from the southern road approach, preferably as morning sunlight highlights its houses and former warehouses behind the harbour. Later in the day these are seen in silhouette against a silvery sea and distant hills. Even more dramatic mountain backgrounds dwarf the whitewashed cottages scattered above the shore-lines at Diabaig and Shieldaig by Loch Torridon to the south of Ullapool.

The remaining groups of Scotland's planned villages all lie south of the Highland line, the fifth one consisting of settlements spread along the trough

Lochinver, Highland. Water-front whitewash in Sutherland's elemental landscape

between Callander and Stonehaven, through Strathallan, Strathmore and the Howe of the Mearns, nicely represented on the Geological Survey Map by the rich brown colouring identifying, again, the Old Red Sandstone. Although the name has a fine ring about it, and doubtless makes the eyes of geologists sparkle, it is a remarkably dull building material. Far more attractive are the yellower sandstones which seem to throw back more sunlight than those of a pink and red hue used in many villages of Angus.

Edzell, a few miles north of Brechin, is a relative latecomer developed by Lord Panmure on the west bank of the Esk in 1839 when it was unimaginatively called Slateford. Entered from the south through a triumphal arch, a long main street of red stone houses leads to the expanse of Edzell Muir, a tree-lined green where the parish church (1819) has an iron belfry. A mild form of 'Balmoralism' about the middle of the century encouraged further development in the village, and modern housing off Church Street is wholly in keeping with the village character. The older village, with its church and former kirkyard, was by Edzell Castle, a mile (1.6km) to the west, an early sixteenth-century tower-house added to over the next hundred years. It was Sir David Lindsay in 1604 who introduced the unique walled garden, where red sandstone was used more imaginatively and decoratively than anywhere else in Scotland, with symbolic decorations in the form of sculptured panels, large indentations, niches, all capped and banded, with a garden-house in one corner, a superb setting for a decoratively formal layout of lawns and shrubs.

Fettercairn, 5 miles (8km) north of Edzell, also has a red stone archway, marking Queen Victoria's visit of 1861. A wide central square is enhanced by the mercat cross from Kincardine, with surrounding houses showing a two-tone appearance, door- and window-dressings being of lighter coloured sandstone than the attractive red of the houses themselves. To the south, Glamis is an old village in a wooded setting by the gates of Glamis Castle, possibly a royal residence since the eleventh century, but now mainly a late seventeenth-century building in splendid ashlar masonry, rich red in its green parkland. The village was rebuilt in the eighteenth century by the Earl of Strathmore, but its most familiar group of cottages in Kirkwynd, now the Angus Folk Museum, dates from the early years of last century. Originally five single-storey cottages with a communal wash-house, they typify in their rubble-walling, slate-slab roofs, stone-flagged floors and small window-openings, the vernacular building of much of Strathmore and Angus. Similar proportions are seen at St Vigean's, near Arbroath, another conservation area village where a group of cottages now houses a folk museum, dominated, like the rest of the village, by a large church of red sandstone on a grassy hill.

Scotland's 'fringe of gold on a green cloth mantle', as James VI described it, is the string of royal burghs along the coast of Fife. Some have become small fisher-towns, some still have the feel of villages, older than and therefore outside the sequences of planned settlements which tend to form the Scottish norm. Trade across the North Sea had brought them prosperity by the sixteenth century and their street patterns today are little changed from four centuries ago. Some villages have become retirement areas, second homes or commuting places, with the National Trust for Scotland playing a vital conservationist role through its 'little houses' scheme which revitalises many seventeenth- and eighteenth-century houses to be seen at St Monance, Pittenweem and the Anstruthers. But it is Crail and Culross which, visually and architecturally, take the palm.

Crail, seen from across the harbour, lifts the spirit. A mosaic of colour, shape and texture rises from sandstone walls by the water, with pink stone, white harling, crow-stepped gables and pantiles on steeply pitched roofs, some slate. In the main street of the village, there is spaciousness, a sturdy tolbooth, more gables, random and rubble and, always, glazing-bars to windows. Culross is even better, not like Crail dependent on the tides or afternoon sunlight to paint its textured surfaces. The streets of Culross reveal its social history: Mid Causey, Little Causey and the Back Causey, all rough-cobbled but crowned with flat stones for pedestrians, are sixteenth century, with Tanhouse Brae running away uphill to the kirk representing the former

197

Crail, Fife. Seventeenth- and eighteenth-century housing by the harbour, showing the rhythm of roof lines, gables and windows. The textural contrasts of bare stone, white harling and pantiles are in evidence

landward access to the harbour. White harling may hide poorer masonry but provides a fine surface to contrast with yellow sandstone door- and window-dressings, and pink pantile roofs. That you cannot see much stone, except on the cobbles, in no way detracts from the boundless delight and visual pleasure in walking the Culross streets on a crisp, bright day in early summer, or in the mellow glow of an autumn afternoon. The Town House of 1626, rebuilt with the tower added in 1783, on the Sandhaven, is the headquarters in Culross for the National Trust for Scotland. Even so, it is worth remembering that most of the 'little houses' which have been so well restored into habitable use were the homes of more prosperous traders, merchants and burghers of the seventeenth century. At Dysart, near Kirkcaldy, many houses from the port's sixteenth- to eighteenth-century importance have been prestigiously revitalised through the 'little houses' scheme. The shore-line and the wandering streets behind it show a felicitous and colourful picture of textured walls, corbelled gables, and pantiled roofs. New buildings have been tastefully incorporated into the scheme.

Falkland, like Culross, has scarcely expanded beyond its seventeenth-century limits, its setting and skyline marked by the turreted towers of its royal palace, built and used by Stuart kings, and splendidly adorning the High Street without overpowering its neighbours. Opposite is Moncrief House, two storeys of finely cut sandstone, with the only thatched roof in the burgh, and dating from 1610. Key House, west of the palace, has steeply pitched gables which also suggest an earlier thatch, now replaced by stone-slate, above white-harled walls. Good restoration of houses in Brunton Street, Sharpe's Close and the Mill Wynd, accompanied by sensible renewal of cobbles, all contribute to the strong ethos of stone that prevails in this first conservation area in Scotland.

Many roads between Cupar and the East Neuk villages have squat, white-painted milestones with place-names picked out in superb lettering, and distance given with unusual precision, even to eighths of a mile (0.2km). Ceres, near Cupar, is frequently named, and, when approached from the east, is seen to sit snugly in a fold of gentle hills as though an English village had been displaced from the wolds of Yorkshire or Lincolnshire. Named after a saint, St Cyr, it is further distinguished by a large green and a seventeenth-century packhorse bridge spanning the Ceres Burn. Surviving groups of stone-built weavers' cottages are reminders of a thriving handloom industry in the eighteenth and early nineteenth centuries, whose relics, together with those of rural life and work, are displayed in the little Folk Museum in the Weigh House, part of the seventeenth-century tolbooth. Solid stone walls of these houses are unharled, but elsewhere in the village colour-washed harl hides the sandstone. Roofs are slate or pantiled and there is little doubt which harmonises better with the stone.

Dysart

Returning to eighteenth-century planned villages, the sixth group consists of mainly 'factory villages' within the influence of Glasgow. Deanston, about 8 miles (13km) north-west of Stirling, in the valley of the Teith, was founded in 1785, with one of the early cotton-mills established when Arkwright's water-frame patents were quashed. The original mill buildings were replaced in 1827 with a larger complex which survives as a distillery. Two rows of houses also survive, on a terrace above the river, and these have been restored by the county council. The later row, on the north side of the street, is distinguished by having upper floors reached by an exterior stair from the footpath arching over a basement area. Buchanan and Arkwright, who designed the village, insisted on gardens being provided behind the houses while whitewash would give the properties a 'cheerful and seemly prospect'. This has now been removed, revealing the sandstone.

South of Glasgow, New Lanark is the most famous of the factory-villages, founded in 1784 by David Dale and Richard Arkwright, with cotton-spinning mills located to harness the water-power of the Falls of Clyde. Built of sandstone, there are four mills, with large blocks of tenement housing strung out along a thickly wooded hillside. The 'New Buildings' were added in 1789 by Dale as a centre-piece, a four-storey block with a bell-tower above the classical middle block. Caithness Row, restored in the 1960s by the New Lanark Association Limited, has the unusual feature at one end of a rounded Counting House, initially built by Robert Owen, whose name as a social

Deanston, Central. Early nineteenth-century mill-village housing. Variety of gable sizes

reformer is so strongly associated with New Lanark. Conservation plans are directed towards revitalising the old village and bringing late eighteenth-century tenement housing up to modern standards. There is still much dereliction to overcome, but the shape and appearance of New Lanark make it, by far, the most outstanding factory-village in Scotland.

Eaglesham, in Renfrewshire, dates from 1796 when the Earl of Eglinton founded it as a small cotton-spinning and weaving town. But the factory he built was soon burned down, and not replaced. Two rows of houses face each other across a very wide green, or meadow, The Orry, directly fronting the street but with long gardens behind. The two rows slope downwards from north to south, gradually diverging, a few of uncovered sandstone but most harled and colour-washed. On the east side of the green, those nearer the top of the hill are larger and more impressive than those nearer the church, and one in Polroon Street still retains its old marriage stone on the lintel. Slate roofs predominate, some of mansard profile, and the sensible method of attaching lamps to house walls rather than leaving them free-standing deserves full praise.

Probably the most rural in appearance of the planned villages is Pitcairngreen, north-west of Perth, established round a bleachfield by Lord Lynedoch at the end of the eighteenth century, with the extraordinary prediction that it might rival Manchester. A variety of houses are spaced round a large green, with about fifty mature trees, mainly oaks, with copper beeches and silver birches planted by local children at the occasion of the present queen's coronation. Use of the green as a football pitch, and by play-groups, comes as rather a relief after the cool, almost inhuman, austerity of so many planned settlements.

Symington, a few miles from Kilmarnock, is as good as any of the villages in an area where development and enlargement of existing settlements has spoiled much. A winding main street, a difference in levels between one part of the village and another, buff sandstone houses with red sandstone dressings, and pleasant groups near the church, give this village character. On the edge of the Carrick Hills of Ayrshire, Straiton starts with more advantages and uses them. Its street gently climbs a hill, with two facing rows of houses, mainly single-storey, many colour-washed, some revealing sombre stone. Those on the south side directly front the pavement, but those opposite have tiny front gardens, just sufficient for a few roses to relieve the grey stone. Date-panels indicate a general rebuilding in the second half of the eighteenth century.

The Silurian slates which underlie most of south-west Scotland are not an attractive building stone, so that it is the situation and shape, rather than the closer view, which distinguishes one place from another. Portpatrick, on the west coast of the Mull of Galloway, developed during the eighteenth and early nineteenth centuries as the nearest port to Ireland, and Rennie was commissioned to build a new harbour in 1821. But heavy Atlantic swells for much of the year gradually caused the abandonment of Portpatrick in favour of the more sheltered Stranraer, leaving the old port to become a holiday village. Most houses disguise their dark grey slate with colour-wash, but the curving crescents either side of Main Street look westwards to the water, the whole naturally attractive setting marred by a huge Victorian hotel on the cliff-top.

Along the lower-lying land between the rolling hills of Galloway and the Solway coast, some villages were founded as burghs of barony during the seventeenth century, and developed the following century as planned communities based on fishing, the coast trade, cotton, linen, or wool-weaving mills. The Isle of Whithorn has suffered a similar fate to Portpatrick, its long-vanished trade with Whitehaven replaced by the seasonal ebb and flow of holiday-makers' boats. Many of its former fishermen's houses are now holiday homes, albeit in a conservation area.

Gatehouse of Fleet, certainly my favourite Galloway village, enjoyed a brief industrial heyday during the decades around 1800, soon after William Murray had laid it out as a linear village serving half a dozen cotton mills, a tannery, a brewery, and a small shipbuilding yard. Robert Mylne designed Cally House for him in 1763, and the place developed at the gates of the big house. Almost wholly colour-washed, with only quoins and dressings to contrast, the main street is dominated by a Victorian clock-tower of granite at the corner by the Murray Arms Hotel, and green lawns by the estate office nearby make a softer foil near the entrance to the policies.

Of the other, smaller settlements on or near the Solway coast, the best part of Auchencairn is just missed by the main road, and enjoys its sloping situation above the bay to its east. Granite, slate and sandstone can all be identified in house walls, even though most of them are hidden behind colour-wash. There is more sandstone at New Abbey, along the coast to the east, where the beautiful red sandstone ruins of Sweetheart Abbey glow above the cottage roofs. A carved stone by one cottage doorway depicts three figures in a boat, thought to commemorate three ladies who, during the building of the abbey in the thirteenth century, ferried some of its stone across the estuary. Another lintel above the former smithy illustrates its motto, inscribed, 'By hammer and hand, All arts do stand.' Stonemasons could well be remembered thus.

So, too, could lead-miners of the seventeenth and eighteenth centuries who lived among the green, rounded Lowther Hills. Leadhills and Wanlockhead are the highest villages in Scotland, the former having further pride in possessing the oldest circulating library in Britain, a 1741 gift of the celebrated Scottish poet, Allan Ramsay, who died there in 1758. Lead-miners' cottages, single-storey, white-washed and as austere as any miners' houses elsewhere, line a sloping, windy street with a church at its higher end, and green silences beyond. The mines ceased in 1914.

Diverse origins characterise the final group of planned settlements, in the Lothian hinterland of Edinburgh. Gifford, Ormiston, Athelstaneford,

Tyninghame, Saltoun and Grangemouth were planned for different reasons. One, Grangemouth, has expanded beyond recognition, and another, Saltoun, has greatly diminished. Of the remainder, Ormiston is East Lothian's best known example, promoted by John Cockburn about 1740 to provide housing for the rural poor who were to be employed in a local brewery, a distillery, and a linen industry, although this was never fully established. The layout has survived, a long main street with a sharp bend at each end closing the outward view. Some bare stonework remains, but much old harling has been replaced by cementwash. Cockburn's aim to have all houses two storeys high was largely carried out, as was his tree-planting, suggesting that the village street was an extension of the avenue in the park.

Gifford, at the northern foot of the Lammermuir Hills, has a fine avenue of mature limes leading from the village centre to the gates of Yester House, with some of the two-storey houses here displaying courses of well-dressed sandstone. Elsewhere in the village, especially in the main street between the cross and the church, white-washed harl, or pale colour-wash, predominates. Although Gifford never had burghal status, it acquired a town cross which stands at the focal point in the village, outside the Town House, formerly the school with its Victorian clock-tower.

Red sandstone and pink pantiles give a glow to Garvald, a few miles east of Gifford, where walls are more exposed, roof lines more varied, the appeal more intimate. So, too, at Stenton, blessed with two greens along its gently curved

Tyninghame, Lothian. Honeyed stone and pantile, eighteenth-century smithy and mid-nineteenth-century house, in an estate village

main street. Each has its well, and the East Green has a tron – scales for weighing wool – recently rebuilt on its original base. Behind are rubble-built cottages of the late seventeenth and eighteenth centuries, some with outside stairs, and roofs of pantile or slate. The saddlebacked and crow-stepped tower of 1525 marks the site of the old church, with eight openings for its doocot, and along the road to the east is the sixteenth-century Rood Well, a circular building with a slate roof – a full-stop at the end of this traditional village, the antithesis of Gifford and its fellows.

Across the A1, Tyninghame is a small-scale reassertion of early nineteenth-century formality, continuing the philanthropic work of eighteenth-century earls of Haddington who planned a village for former retainers on the Tyninghame estates. In the 1830s the village was rebuilt and extended, with single-storey houses of good quality ashlared sandstone around courtyards, together with a school-house, hall and post office. Well-matured woodlands add to the ideal of a picturesque village. In contrast, Athelstaneford represents a model village of late eighteenth-century date promoted by landowner Sir David Kinloch. Single-storey cottages line both sides of one street along a whinstone ridge, with a smithy at the eastern end. Pantiled roofs rise above eaves which are only 6 or 7ft (1.8 or 2.1m) from the ground, so that some doors are higher than, and many windows almost reach, the eaves. The two-room smallest cottages cost £15–£20 to build, the larger ones much more, but the agricultural labourers for whom the houses were built had 38-year leases, and shared 100 acres (40ha) of good land at a moderate rent, enabling them to be almost completely self-supporting. Sir John Sinclair was so impressed as to comment: 'There is no village where of late years the inhabitants have improved more in comfort and convenience than in Athelstaneford.'

On the Forth coast, almost opposite the southern shore of the East Neuk, Dirleton in medieval times consisted of a late Norman castle centred on its massive, circular drum tower, and little else. Parish church and main settlement at Gullane were, by the seventeenth century, being badly affected by sand, and the heart of the village moved inland to its present site, developing round a green north of Dirleton castle in the seventeenth and eighteenth centuries. Village houses are grouped informally round the green, early ones of rubble walls and pantile roofs, Georgian ones more substantial and of dressed stone, with the nineteenth century represented by decorated Gothic dormers and chimneys of Vine Cottage. The sandstone used throughout ensures unity, the green between castle and seventeenth-century church provides spaciousness, all making one of Scotland's most English-looking villages.

Pencaitland's magnificent church, mainly of the sixteenth and seventeenth centuries, and the two tiny offertory houses in its churchyard are sufficient to justify including in this survey the twin villages of Easter and Wester Pencaitland on either side of the wooded River Tyne. Both parts of the village

Wester Pencaitland, Lothian. Seventeenth-century market cross and nineteenth-century houses in yellow-brown sandstone; slate roofs

Denholm, Border. Late eighteenth-century 'green' village of English appearance

contain good houses of grey stone, and the statue of a schoolboy looks down from above the school-porch, a significant reference to Scottish pride in education.

Denholm, near Hawick, has a huge central green, beautifully kept, with an ornate memorial to the poet and oriental scholar, John Leyden, but most of the houses round the green were part of this village planned for stocking-weavers, a pleasant mixture of two- and three-storey buildings set against hedgerows and hillsides of the Teviot valley.

11

A Personal Choice

When, in 1958, John Betjeman produced his *Guide to English Parish Churches*, among the criteria justifying the inclusion of a church was that it should contain one object 'which, regardless of date, was aesthetically worth bicycling twelve miles against the wind to see'. Although no such criterion is introduced into the list of villages which follows, those named are of particular merit in one way or another, as good representatives of stone villages from all the areas reviewed. They are not necessarily picturesque, pretty, or even charming, although many undoubtedly are, and the inclusion of any village on the list can be justified on one or more grounds. It may be the quality or variety of individual houses, the 'villagescape' of groups of buildings either by the church, around a green, along a street or by a bridge. In some cases the setting may be a dominant factor, but throughout it is the stone which dictates the character and creates the sense of place. I must emphasise that the list is purely a personal one and in no way is it intended to be definitive. Here, then, are my hundred English villages, with twenty-five from Wales and Scotland together.

2   LURE OF THE LIMESTONE

Abbotsbury, Dorset   *8ml 13km NW of Weymouth*
Near, but not on the coast. Golden limestone and thatch. Has largely belonged to one family since Dissolution of Monasteries. Lived in, worked in, cared for, and consistently attractive.

Barnack, Cambridgeshire   *3ml4km SE of Stamford*
Honeyed stone from famous quarries imparts unity to a straggling village.
Hills and hollows whence it came look like giants' graves.

Barnwell, Northamptonshire   *2ml4km S of Oundle*
A stream down the middle, green verges, an avenue of elms, houses down each
side, a flourish of finials and a church on a hill.

Bibury, Gloucestershire   *7ml11km NE of Cirencester*
Ducks on the Coln's clear waters attract summer crowds; Arlington Row is
superb, gabled and textured. Elegant bale tombs in the churchyard should not
be missed.

Bledington, Gloucestershire   *4ml6km SE of Stow-on-the-Wold*
Large, irregular green carpeting to cottages, and intersected by a winding
stream. Informal, spacious, peaceful.

Blockley, Gloucestershire   *3ml5km NW of Moreton-in-Marsh*
Echoes of industry still linger in this secluded valley-village. Fine ashlar gives
a prosperous air to the houses, some of them having been converted from silk-
mills.

Burton Bradstock, Dorset   *3ml4km SE of Bridport*
At the western end of the Chesil Beach; stone, thatch, some colour-wash, gaily
painted doors, streets and lanes make an intricate network, and every prospect
pleases.

Castle Combe, Wiltshire   *5ml9km NW of Chippenham*
Near Chippenham, but no main road ventures into the By Brook valley. Three
streets meet at the nucleus, Market Cross and church. One comes by the
brook, one down a hill, and the third goes nowhere. Perfection in honeyed
stone.

Chilmark, Wiltshire   *8ml12km W of Wilton*
Cosy in the Nadder valley, with grey stone, thatched houses, a small stream,
sheltered by beeches and downs.

Collyweston, Northamptonshire   *3ml5km SW of Stamford*
This large attractive village shows variety of grey stone houses, roofed with
the famous local slates.

Corfe Castle, Dorset   *4ml6km SE of Wareham*
Contrasts in house sizes, shapes, textures, yet unified by the focal dominance of

208

the castle. Best views from the churchyard, looking down West Street. A subtle symphony in stone.

Coxwold, North Yorkshire   *5ml8km N of Easingwold*
This street-village climbs a hill to its octagonal towered church. Mellow stone cottages line grass verges and cobbles; and trees are an attractive foil. Look east from the lychgate for afternoon delight.

Duddington, Northamptonshire   *5ml8km SW of Stamford*
A street of attractive eighteenth-century houses winds down a hill to the old bridge across the Welland, and the watermill nearby.

Easton on the Hill, Northamptonshire   *2ml3km SW of Stamford*
Good views within the village, with streets at slightly different levels providing variety of perspectives and angles on the unifying stone.

Filkins, Oxfordshire   *4ml6km NE of Lechlade*
This has stone not only for houses and roofs but also as upright slabs for garden walls. Some houses have carved figures of shepherds and stonemasons, appropriate in the Cotswold area.

Fulbeck, Lincolnshire   *9ml15km N of Grantham*
Houses of pale Ancaster stone loosely scattered round a green and along the lanes to Low Fields.

Geddington, Northamptonshire   *3ml5km NE of Kettering*
The best surviving Eleanor Cross graces a charming village square. Cool grey stone, gables, some thatch, a tall-spired church and a medieval stone bridge across the willowy River Ise.

Greatford, Lincolnshire   *5ml8km NE of Stamford*
Linear village 10 miles NW of Peterborough. Handsome farm groups, neat stone houses, and whimsical carved stones in front gardens.

Guiting Power, Gloucestershire   *6ml10km W of Stow-on-the-Wold*
Surrounded by well-spaced parkland trees. New housing harmonises with the old, with gables, stone roofs, and an obviously cared-for appearance.

Hanslope, Buckinghamshire   *5ml8km NW of Newport Pagnell*
Warm buff seventeenth-century stone cottages, well restored, with a nice blend of Georgian houses, make an attractive street to the NE of the finest steeple in Buckinghamshire.

Hovingham, North Yorkshire   *8ml12km W of Malton*
Cool limestone, warm-pink pantile, greens, a clear stream, and two broad streets, within the unifying influence of the Worsley estate. Spacious and satisfying, with mature trees.

Ketton, Leicestershire   *4ml6km SW of Stamford*
Probably the best of the quarry villages, with a rich variety of creamy-grey stone houses from the seventeenth to nineteenth centuries, mainly bordering paths and streets. Splendid headstones by the churchyard path.

Little Barrington, Gloucestershire   *3ml5km W of Burford*
Tiny stream flows down a green hollow, formerly the quarry that yielded the golden stone of the stylish cottages which now fringe it.

Melbury Osmond, Dorset   *5ml8km S of Yeovil*
A gently curving hill of houses descends to a stream in the quiet heart of rural north Dorset.

Mells, Somerset   *3ml5km W of Frome*
Blessed with numerous little greens, mature trees, a gentle valley setting; houses and cottages of grey limestone loosely scattered, except in Church Street, where a medieval bishop started to build a new town.

Powerstock, Dorset   *4ml6km NE of Bridport*
Buff-grey cottages at different levels, gardens, orchards and deep lanes.

Sherston, Wiltshire   *5ml8km W of Malmesbury*
Broad rectangular main street, a former Market Place, bordered by Cotswold-style houses of cool, grey stone.

Snowshill, Gloucestershire   *3ml4km S of Broadway*
Hill-perched on the Cotswold escarpment may merit its wintry name but belies its summer cosiness. Gables, dormers, mullions, lintels, honey-gold stone, centred on church and green, with gentle slopes, and hills beyond.

Stanton, Gloucestershire   *3ml4km SW of Broadway*
Just off the A46 midway between Cheltenham and Evesham, sheltering below the escarpment. Pure and perfect Cotswold in a largely twentieth-century restoration, lovingly carried out. The modern council housing is excellent too.

Stoke Abbot, Dorset   *2ml3km W of Beaminster*
Sheltered, secluded, linear, with a curve, flower-bedecked, with nothing dominating, nothing ostentatious.

Taynton, Oxfordshire   *2km NW of Burford*
In the Windrush valley, source of some of the finest Cotswold oolite. Variety of house-types and dates emphasise that this was a working village.

3   ALONG THE LIAS

Adderbury, Oxfordshire   *3ml/5km S of Banbury*
Manor-house, green, rust-coloured thatched cottages interspersed with neat Georgian houses.

Aynho, Northamptonshire   *6ml/9km SE of Banbury*
Main road village on a hill SE of Banbury. Immaculate in appearance, needs sunlight to warm its pearl-grey stone.

Bramham, West Yorkshire   *4ml/6km S of Wetherby*
Short mazy lanes of creamy limestone cottages, pink pantiles, small windows; a place for sauntering in afternoon sunlight.

Deddington, Oxfordshire   *6ml/9km S of Oxford*
Large market square off main road, good houses and cottages tucked away behind stone walls.

East Coker, Somerset   *3ml/4km SW of Yeovil*
Golden stone, thatch, small bridges across a stream, colourful gardens, high-banked lanes and memories of T. S. Eliot.

Hinton St George, Somerset   *2ml/4km NW of Crewkerne*
Cared for, cossetted, charming, with a variety of shapes, sizes and ages of cottages and houses.

Hooton Pagnell, South Yorkshire   *7ml/11km NW of Doncaster*
Grey stone houses, pantile-roofed; hill-stepping produces pleasing patterns;

small green, Butter Cross, proud church and Hall provide contrasts and history.

Hornton, Oxfordshire   *5m/8km NW of Banbury*
Iron-tinted cottages down a hill; small green, tall trees, informal and inviting.

Lyddington, Leicestershire   *2m/3km S of Uppingham*
Loveliest of linear villages, with many sizes of houses and cottages directly fronting street. Two-toned Bay House and Bede House outstanding. Scarcely a discordant note.

Montacute, Somerset   *4m/6km W of Yeovil*
Golden Ham stone, mullions, red tiles, interesting street plan, superb Elizabethan mansion.

Queen Camel, Somerset   *2km SW of Sparkford*
Cool grey stone along one main street. Stone causeway between cottage rows to handsome church.

Warmington, Warwickshire   *5m/8km NW of Banbury*
Houses of rust-coloured stone aloofly surround a spacious, manicured green. Roofs of stone, slate, thatch; white-painted woodwork. Too-formal Town Pool with friendly ducks.

West Tanfield, North Yorkshire   *5m/8km NW of Ripon*
Perfect composition in view from river bridge. Church, gatehouse-tower, cottages, gardens.

Wroxton, Oxfordshire   *3m/5km W of Banbury*
Steep grassy banks line the main street. Thatched cottages of Hornton stone; cobbled causeway to church. Roses and honeysuckle.

4   MOUNTAIN LIMESTONE

Alstonefield, Staffordshire   *6m/10km NW of Ashbourne*
Lively variety among network of lanes, with two small greens and tall trees.

Arncliffe, North Yorkshire   *7m/11km NW of Grassington*
Seventeenth- and eighteenth-century houses by a green: limestone scars etch green hillsides beyond. Farms and barns well integrated into village scene.

Bonsall, Derbyshire   *2ml3km SW of Matlock*
Large village deserving leisurely exploration. Good group round square, industrial overtones throughout. Austere but attractive.

Elton, Derbyshire   *5ml8km W of Matlock*
Unusual, limestone on one side of street, gritstone on the other.

Hartington, Derbyshire   *9ml15km N of Ashbourne*
Large market place, dignified houses, many three-storeyed, in cool grey stone.

Linton-in-Craven, North Yorkshire   *1m S of Grassington*
Three bridges, a ford and stepping-stones, across stream bisecting a green. Splendid houses around; everything delights the eye.

Middleton by Youlgreave, Derbyshire   *2km SW of Youlgreave*
Early nineteenth-century estate village, neat groups round triangular space, excellent ranges of farm buildings, and the Bradford valley below.

Taddington, Derbyshire   *5ml8km W of Bakewell*
Linear, on a shelf, with good views from road above. Variety in styles and sizes of houses, unity of limestone, contrasts with gritstone dressings.

5   CHALK, FLINT, PEBBLES AND BOULDERS

Blakeney, Norfolk   *5ml7km NW of Holt*
A glow of flint and brick down High Street, attractive groups along the Quay, and round cosy courtyards.

Brancaster, Norfolk   *4ml6km W of Burnham Market*
Brick and flint cottages line one gently curving street, highlighted by white wooden doors and shallow window frames.

Cley, Norfolk   *4ml6km NW of Holt*
Colour, texture, flint and brick in a salty, bracing setting of sea-views and soaring skies.

Compton Bassett, Wiltshire   *3ml4km E of Calne*
Good examples of chalk cottages, with overhanging thatch, below the downs.

Hambleden, Buckinghamshire   *3ml5km NE of Henley-on-Thames*
Mainly a mid-Victorian estate village, with flint and brick cottages and a stream, among the Chilterns.

Sydling St Nicholas, Dorset   *2ml4km NE of Maiden Newton*
Thatched cottages of banded flint and stone in gently curving High Street in a secluded valley setting.

Uffington, Oxfordshire   *4ml7km S of Faringdon*
Six lanes converge on this sprawling village, where some houses and cottages show walls of large chalk blocks, usually brick-dressed.

Wereham, Norfolk   *2ml3km NW of Stoke Ferry*
A pleasant mixture of materials, flint and brick, dark carstone, pale colour-wash, giving a lively visual and textural variety.

6   SANDSTONE VILLAGES OF VALES AND DOWNS

Bamburgh, Northumberland   *5ml7km E of Belford*
Coastal village dominated by a grand castle. Grey stone cottages facing small green, with the sea out of sight.

Cardington, Shropshire   *4ml6km E of Church Stretton*
Neat cottage groups near the church, dormered windows, delightful gardens, fine trees, farm buildings, among Shropshire hills.

Danby, North Yorkshire   *12ml19km W of Whitby*
Sheep-grazed greens in a moorland setting. Trees grace good cottage groups. Colourful, spacious, airy, clean.

East Quantoxhead, Somerset   *4ml6km E of Watchet*
Scattered cottages of purple-brown rubble; delightful duck pond. Fine group of church, Court House, and farm buildings.

Elsdon, Northumberland.   *3ml5km E of Otterburn*
Dignified grey stone, tree-shaded church, fourteenth-century pele tower, and a huge green.

Hutton-le-Hole, North Yorkshire   *2ml4km N of Kirkbymoorside*
Moorland gem, sheepy greens, a lively stream, well-spaced cottages of mellow stone, pink-roofed and pert, an excellent Folk Museum, and a good car park.

Kirkoswald, Cumbria   *7ml11km N of Penrith*
Warm pink stone in a hill-climbing linear village. Colour-wash, cobbles, sand-stone flags, a small graceful square, above the Eden Valley.

Milburn, Cumbria   *6ml10km N of Appleby*
An outstanding 'green' village in a superb setting. Colour-wash, painted dressings, but plenty of warm red stone on green Pennine slopes.

Osmotherley, North Yorkshire   *6ml10km NE of Northallerton*
As warm, colourful and friendly as its name suggests. Grey-brown stone, pink pantiles, cobbled pavements, grass verges, market cross and stone table, and the moors beyond.

Robin Hood's Bay, North Yorkshire   *5ml8km SE of Whitby*
Unforgettable, terraced and tiered on a steep cliff, tumbled roofs and gables, tightly-clustered cottages, cobbles, tiny gardens, endless steps and the restless sea.

Temple Sowerby, Cumbria   *6ml10km NW of Appleby*
Plenty of warm pink sandstone, attractive green; cared for and colourful.

(overleaf)————————————————————————————————

Mankinholes, West Yorkshire. Fine seventeenth-century vernacular building in the Calder valley

7 THE OLDER SANDSTONES

Askrigg, North Yorkshire *4ml6km NW of Aysgarth*
Former market centre, retains its cross, pump, bull ring. Mainly linear, on a curving rise, dignified with elegant, three-storey houses and inns. Fascinating little corners.

Bainbridge, North Yorkshire *4ml6km E of Hawes*
Superb setting, with unpretentious cottages of grey-brown stone bordering large well-kept green. Ideally appreciated in view from Roman fort to east.

Blanchland, Northumberland *9ml14km S of Hexham*
Mid-eighteenth-century planned village in upper Derwent valley. Stone cottages round broad cobbled courtyards; monastic gatehouse and refectory integral with villagescape. Perfect in setting, layout and detail. Not to be missed!

Chipping, Lancashire *4ml6km NE of Longridge*
Former market centre. Good seventeenth- and eighteenth-century houses, rich details, pleasant courtyards and cobbles. Full of texture and visual appeal.

Cromford, Derbyshire *2ml3km N of Wirksworth*
Late-eighteenth-century industrial village, unified by gritstone, planned with enlightenment, full of architectural details and interest.

Downham, Lancashire *3ml5km NE of Clitheroe*
Straggles down a hill, with fine views to Pendle country. Small green, good variety of cottages and houses.

Edensor, Derbyshire *2ml4km E of Bakewell*
Planned picturesqueness in the grand manner. Victorian, Norman, Tudor, Swiss, Gothic, all in splendid dark stone, with exuberant detail, in parkland setting.

Eyam, Derbyshire *5ml8km N of Bakewell*
Large, stylish Peakland village with fine variety of houses showing traditional seventeenth- and eighteenth-century local building styles. Poignant memories persist.

Heptonstall, West Yorkshire *1km NW of Hebden Bridge*
Hilltop village, austerely handsome, a showpiece survival of eighteenth- and nineteenth-century domestic weaving community. Gritstone houses and cottages, in terraces and folds, flagged causeways and fine views across wall-stitched valleys to green hillsides.

Longnor, Staffordshire *6ml9km SE of Buxton*
Breezy, spacious upland village, cobbles, flags, dark sandstone houses and cottages, three-storeyed dignity.

Luddenden, West Yorkshire *2ml3km E of Mytholmroyd*
Compact, crammed, hilly, exciting, with memories of cottage industries.

Mankinholes, West Yorkshire *2ml3km E of Todmorden*
Tiny, remote, memorable, rich in seventeenth-century vernacular buildings; cobbles, and fine stone water troughs for packhorse trains.

Ribchester, Lancashire *5ml8km N of Blackburn*
Handloom weavers' village, houses reflect prosperity of 1790–1825. Dark stone, date-panels, delightful details and setting.

Ripley, North Yorkshire *3ml5km N of Harrogate*
Perfect early Victorian estate village: cobbled square with stocks and cross, grass verges, trees, two-storey houses with splendid detail. Neat little school, flamboyant 'Hotel de Ville'.

Romaldkirk, Co Durham *5ml8km NW of Barnard Castle*
Enjoys many greens. Cottages pleasantly dispersed informally. Sizes, shapes, angles and gables create variety and interest. Best of the Teesdale villages.

Staindrop, Co Durham *5ml9km NE of Barnard Castle*
Long green-village of sandstone houses, pantiled and colour-washed. Delightful details, some excellent modern building keeps the harmony.

Waddington, Lancashire *2ml3km NW of Clitheroe*
Brook-blessed, with gardens, flowers, trees a perfect foil to dark stone cottages in rows and small squares.

8   THE HARDEST ROCKS

Altarnun, Cornwall   *7ml11km W of Launceston*
A single-street village climbing a hill, with cottages of granite, slate, some with slate-hanging. Dark grey and brown, some colour-wash, white woodwork. Unostentatious harmony.

Charlestown, Cornwall   *1m SE of St Austell*
A colour-washed slate-stone gem above Smeaton's late-eighteenth-century harbour.

Delabole, Cornwall   *2ml4km W of Camelford*
Austere quarry village, grey or blue-green slate, sliced, slabbed, often colour-washed, close to the biggest hole in Britain.

Elterwater, Cumbria   *3ml5km W of Ambleside*
The best slate village in the Lake District. Naked rock, coursed, sharp, grey-green stone, splendidly irregular quoins and lintels, but beautifully graded roofs.

Grasmere, Cumbria   *3ml5km NW of Ambleside*
Stylish Victorian villas and boarding-houses, older cottages, modern in-fill, in fascinating harmonies of grey-purple slate encircled by friendly green hills.

Hawkshead, Cumbria   *4ml7km S of Ambleside*
Snug squares, quiet courtyards, cobbles, canopied porches, outside stairways, slate-hanging, colour-washed rendering. A delight of shapes, surfaces, corners, angles, surprises, and one of the best churchyard views in England.

Luxulyan, Cornwall *4ml7km NE of St Austell*
Hillside village of granite, where the massive, austere stone does not overwhelm. Houses and cottages at different levels; cobbles, steps, gables, angles, surfaces make for visual and textural delight.

Port Isaac, Cornwall *5ml8km N of Wadebridge*
Slate-hanging and colour-wash in steep narrow streets. Compact and cosy.

Troutbeck, Cumbria *3ml5km N of Windermere*
Linear, lovely and full of surprises. Farms, barns, houses, cottages, walls, flowers, springs. Richly rewarding, and must be savoured slowly to appreciate its vernacular variety.

Woodhouse Eaves, Leicestershire *4ml6km S of Loughborough*
Rather scattered, but a Midland surprise. Cottages of many-tinted Charnwood Forest slate-stone, mainly brown or blue-grey. Nicely offset by trees and colourful gardens.

Zennor, Cornwall *4ml7km W of St Ives*
Granite boulders by the lane, granite houses clustered by the church in a windswept, treeless landscape.

9   WALES

Aberdovey, Gwynedd *9ml14km W of Machynlleth*
This small resort on the north shore of the Dovey estuary is clean, breezy and consistently attractive. The stone may be hidden beneath colour-wash but the seaside setting is superb.

Beddgelert, Gwynedd *12ml19km SE of Caernarfon*
Grey slate houses by a bridge and rocky river, in a wooded valley, present a compact picture.

Corris, Gwynedd   *4ml7km N of Machynlleth*
Slate rules all in this quarry village, yet is not gloomily overpowering. Grey courses in house walls, lumpy quoins and garden fences of upright slates like gapped teeth.

Dyffryn Ardudwy, Gwynedd   *5ml8km N of Barmouth*
Colour-wash, but plenty of massive chunks of slate in the walls. Splendidly primitive in appearance.

Maentwrog, Gwynedd   *3ml4km W of Ffestiniog*
A slate village, tiered with taste along a hillside, backed by cliffs and trees.

Meifod, Powys   *4ml7km S of Llanfyllin*
In the broad valley of the River Vyrnwy, this street-village is of brown-grey slate-stone, with many good Georgian houses.

Nevern, Dyfed   *2ml3km E of Newport*
Small, secluded; some colour-wash, mill groups, good slate headstones and Celtic cross in churchyard.

Skenfrith, Gwent   *6ml9km NW of Monmouth*
Its thirteenth-century castle looks across gardens and up the street to the sturdy church. More green with grass than sombre with stone.

Solva, Dyfed   *3ml5km E of St David's*
Fine village on coastal inlet with close-grouped buildings in the valley and the enlarging village on the hill above. Chapels, mills, and plenty of carparking by the former harbour.

Talgarth, Powys   *7ml11km SW of Hay-on-Wye*
Distinguished by a fortified tower overlooking the small square, interesting groups of buildings, and the character of a close-knit community.

Tremadog, Gwynedd   *1m N of Porthmadog*
The most rewarding planned village in Wales: slate used elegantly and functionally in a spacious setting frowned upon by tree-covered cliffs.

Trevine, Dyfed   *7ml11km NE of St David's*
Undistinguished architecture but tremendous stone presence through huge outcrops of rock where a village green should be.

10   SCOTLAND

Athelstaneford, Lothian   *3ml 4km NE of Haddington*
A one-street village of mainly single-storey cottages with pantiled roofs.
When built about 1790 the houses cost £15–£20 each and had large gardens
behind.

Ceres, Fife   *3ml 4km SE of Cupar*
The most 'English' of the Fife villages, with large green, houses of sandstone
irregularly grouped, and a packhorse bridge in pleasant rolling country.

Crail, Fife   *2ml 4km SW of Fife Ness*
Large fishing village with delightful streets and house-groups, especially by
the harbour. Splendid villagescape throughout, focused on sturdy tolbooth of
*c*1600.

Deanston, Central   *1m W of Doune*
Across the River Teith from Doune, distinguished not so much by its distillery
as by the nineteenth-century mill-workers' houses in the main street. Rising
steps to doors create good shadow-patterns.

Dornoch, Highland   *12ml 19km E of Bonar Bridge*
Cathedral-resort village on Sutherland's east coast. Yellow sandstone, broad
streets and roses in the garden.

Eaglesham, Strathclyde   *4ml 7km SW of East Kilbride*
Planned as a factory village, with a very wide green, and elegant houses of freestone down each side. They're all still there, with the trees and stream, but the
rows were too far apart to be neighbourly. Fascinating, attractive conservation
village.

Fordyce, Grampian   *3ml 4km SW of Portsoy*
Red sandstone cottages front on to winding lanes, all of which lead to the tiny sixteenth-century castle and the old Kirk beyond. Happily, disorderly organic.

Fowlis Wester, Tayside   *4ml 7km E of Crieff*
Completely rural in setting and character. Small green, small houses and cottages, a natural rather than a planned village.

Gardenstown, Grampian   *6ml 9km E of Macduff*
Sensationally steep lanes fall down cliffs to the harbour. Tiered, terraced and tortuous: Scotland's equivalent to Robin Hood's Bay or Clovelly.

New Lanark, Strathclyde   *1km S of Lanark*
On the outskirts of Lanark, by the banks of the Clyde, this is the most outstanding industrial village in Scotland. Now being restored, and not to be missed on any account.

Pencaitland, Lothian   *4ml 6km SE of Tranent*
The Tyne Water separates the Easter and Wester parts of this delightful village. Everything pleases; great variety of stone houses, fine church, and fascinating churchyard.

Straiton, Strathclyde   *6ml 10km SE of Maybole*
On the Water of Girvan this eighteenth-century village climbs a hill. Small, colourful front gardens give it a distinction appropriate to its beautiful setting.

Ullapool, Highland   *E shore of Loch Broom*
Fishing port and resort on the east shore of Loch Broom; memorable in its peninsular situation, planned in 1788 for the British Fisheries Society, the street lay-out needs to be seen at close quarters. The view from the A835 southern approach is worth the long journey to the far north-west.

Bibliography

Many topographical books of a general nature have been consulted, some no longer in print. In addition the county volumes in 'The Making of the English Landscape' series (Hodder and Stoughton) and the 'Regions of Britain' series (Eyre Methuen) have been particularly useful. Pevsner's 'The Buildings of England' series is unlikely to be surpassed for fifty years. Later volumes included a section on Building Materials, and the first volumes for Wales and Scotland have appeared. The following list contains more specialised works.

Barley, M. W., *The English Farmhouse & Cottage* (Routledge & Kegan Paul, 1961, 1976)

Beresford, M. W., *Lost Villages of England* (Lutterworth, 1954)

Bourne, G., *Change in the Village* (Duckworth, 1912)

Brill, E. J., *Life & Tradition on the Cotswolds* (Dent, 1973)

—— *Cotswold Crafts* (Readers Union, 1977)

Brown, R. and J., *The English Country Cottage* (Hale, 1979)

Brunskill, R. W., *Illustrated Handbook of Vernacular Architecture* (Faber & Faber, 1978)

—— *Vernacular Architecture of the Lake Counties: A Field Handbook* (Faber & Faber, 1974)

—— *Traditional Buildings of Britain: An Introduction to Vernacular Architecture* (Gollancz, 1981)

Clifton-Taylor, A., *The Pattern of English Building* (Faber & Faber, 1972)

Clifton-Taylor, A. and Ireson, A. S., *English Stone Building* (Gollancz, 1983)

Cobbett, W., *Rural Rides* (Everyman, 1957)

Darley, G., *Villages of Vision* (Architect Press, 1975)

Davey, N., *Building Stones of England & Wales* (Bedford Square, 1976)

Defoe, D., *A Tour Through the Whole Island of Great Britain* (Penguin, 1971)

Hadfield, J. (ed), *The Shell Book of English Villages* (Michael Joseph, 1980)

Harrison, J. A. C., *Old Stone Buildings: Buying, Extending, Renovating* (David & Charles, 1982)

Hawkes, J., *A Land* (David & Charles, 1978)

Hoskins, W. G. and Stamp, Dudley, *The Common Lands of England & Wales* (Collins, 1963)

Hudson, K., *The Fashionable Stone* (Adams & Dart, 1971)

Massingham, H. J., *Cotswold Country* (Batsford, 1937)

Millward, R. and Robinson, A., *Landscapes of North Wales* (David & Charles, 1978)

Morris, C. (ed), *The Journeys of Celia Fiennes* (Cresset, 1947)

Muir, R., *The English Village* (Thames & Hudson, 1980)

Penoyre, J. and J., *Houses in the Landscape: A Regional Study of Vernacular Building Styles in England & Wales* (Faber & Faber, 1978)

Phillipson, N. T. and Mitchison, R. (ed) *Scotland in the Age of Improvement* (Edinburgh U.P., 1970)

Porter, J., *The Making of the Central Pennines* (Moorland, 1980)

Prentice, R. (ed), *The National Trust for Scotland Guide* (Cape, 1981)

Priestley, J. B., *English Journey* (Heinemann, 1934)

Prizeman, J., *Your House: The Outside View* (Hutchinson, 1975)

Raistrick, A., *Buildings in the Yorkshire Dales* (Dalesman, 1976)

Rollinson, W., *Life & Tradition in the Lake District* (Dent, 1974)

Rowley, T., *Villages in the Landscape* (Dent, 1978)

Tarn, J. N., *The Peak District National Park – Its Architecture* (Peak Planning Bd, no date)

Timmins, J. G., *Handloom Weavers' Cottages in Central Lancashire* (University of Lancaster, 1977)

Trinder, B., *The Making of the Industrial Landscape* (Dent, 1982)

Trueman, A. E., *Geology & Scenery in England & Wales* (Penguin, 1971)

Whittow, J. B., *Geology & Scenery in Scotland* (Penguin, 1977)

Woodforde, J., *The Truth About Cottages* (Routledge & Kegan Paul, 1979)

—— *Georgian Houses for All* (Routledge & Kegan Paul, 1978)

Bainbridge Wensleydale

Index

Figures in *italics* indicate illustrations